On The Homefront

A Family Survival Guide

Katrina L. Cassel

CPH
SAINT LOUIS

Copyright © 1999 Concordia Publishing House
3558 S. Jefferson Avenue, St. Louis, MO 63118-3968
Manufactured in the United States of America

Library of Congress Cataloging-in-Publication Data
Cassel, Katrina L., 1962-
On the homefront : a family survival guide/ Katrina L. Cassel.
p. cm.
Summary: Looks at various types of families, parents, siblings that exist today,
and God's plans for them. Includes Biblical passages.
ISBN 0-570-07000-7
1. Family--Juvenile literature. 2. Family--Religious aspects--Christianity--
Juvenile literature. 3. Teenagers--Family relationships--Juvenile literature.
4.Preteens--Family relations--Juvenile literature (1.Family--Religious aspects--
Christianity. 2. Family life--religious aspects--Christianity. 3.Christian life.) I.
Title.
HQ744. C37 2000
306.85--dc21   99-047327

1 2 3 4 5 6 7 8 9 10   09 08 07 06 05 04 03 02 01 00

To the family I grew up in—Mom, Ken, and Lou;
and to the family I am a part of now—my husband
Rick, and children Tyler, Jessica, Jeff, and Adam.

To all the kids who helped with this book. May God
bless your families and fill them with His love and joy.

Table of Contents

INTRODUCTION

What do you think of when someone says "family"? Many different pictures might come into your mind—and they may all be right. Not all families are the same.

This book will help you take a look at your own family. In it, we will look at how families have changed through the years and how they are still the same. We also will look at the challenges of nontraditional families.

You will meet several people your age from different kinds of families. They took the time to share with me what makes their families different, the same, and special. Even though they are from different kinds of families, they share many of the same interests, activities, and feelings.

In this book you will learn some skills to help you understand your parents and communicate with them better. We will look at how to fight fairly with siblings and how to improve your relationships with them. These skills will help you no matter what kind of family you have.

No matter what your family is like, God cares about you. He knows all about your family—He created it! He understands the challenges you face and the fun you have, and stays with you through both. He has a wonderful plan for you (see Jeremiah 29:11), a plan that started long ago when He sent His Son, Jesus, to die on the cross to forgive your sins.

Throughout this book I talk about "parents." If you live with someone other than your own parents, that's okay. Just substitute their names for the word "parents" and keep reading. This book is for you!

Katrina L. Cassel

A Look at Families Today

Chapter 1

This Is a Family?

What do you think of when someone says the word "family"? Do you picture a dad, mom, and two children all laughing and having fun together, or do you picture a different sort of family—maybe your own? If you don't have a traditional family of four, you're not alone! In this chapter, we will look at different types of family units.

> Logan's book bag hit the floor with a thud. He dropped to his bed, lay back, and turned his CD player up full blast. Even that didn't drown out the sounds from below, the sounds of his four younger sisters arguing about whose turn it was to start supper and whose turn it was to vacuum.
>
> Rachel, the oldest of the girls, burst into Logan's room unannounced. "They won't help me again. The house is a mess and Mom will be home in an hour."
>
> "That's your problem. You're the one in trouble if things aren't done when Mom gets home," Logan said.
>
> "How come you don't have to help?" Rachel whined. "It's not fair. You're just goofing off."
>
> "I have to work tonight and I have to get my homework done. If you'd get out of my room, I could do it," Logan said.
>
> Rachel left and Logan reluctantly sat up and dug his math book out of his book bag. "I wonder what it'd be like to come home to a normal family," he wondered. "I wish Dad were still here."

Your Turn

Are you happy with your family, or discontent like Logan? All of us wish at some time in our lives that we could change our family situation. But since we can't, the best thing is to accept the families we have. Let's take a look at families today.

What Is a Family?

The dictionary gives several different definitions for family. One is, "A group of individuals living under one roof and usually under one head." Another definition is, "The basic unit in society having as its nucleus two or more adults living together and cooperating in the care and rearing of their own or adopted children."

Neither of these definitions is entirely satisfactory. Many groups of individuals live together, but that doesn't make them a family. And two or more adults living together raising children isn't a family in God's eyes, unless they are a married man and woman.

God's plan is for a man and a woman to leave their own families, unite in marriage and form a new family unit (Genesis 2:20–24). Unfortunately, that doesn't always happen today. Not all families have two adults. Children aren't always raised by their parents. But just because your family doesn't match God's original plan, it doesn't mean God doesn't love you or think you're important. Through Jesus' death and resurrection, He made you a part of His family. He gives you plenty of people to love and accept you as family here on earth. And He has His own plan for a family of your own in the future.

Different Kinds of Families

It would be hard to write a definition of a family that fits all of the possible family units. Let's look at a few of the possible family combinations.

- Two parents in their first marriage raising biological children.

- Two parents in their first marriage raising adopted or foster children.

- Two parents in their first marriage raising a combination of adopted, foster, and biological children.

- Two married adults with no children.

- Two parents, one or both married before, with children from previous marriages.

- Two parents, one or both married before, with children from this marriage.

- Two parents, one or both married before, with a combination of children from all marriages.

- Two adults, one or both married before, with no children.

- A single mom raising biological or adopted children.

- A single dad raising biological or adopted children.

- One or two grandparents raising their grand-children.

- Uncles and aunts raising nieces and nephews.

These are only some of the possible combinations that make up a family. You can probably think of more.

Not All Families Are the Same

Some special people helped me with this book. They are real kids from real families like yours. You will read their comments throughout the book. Let me introduce them to you so when you read what they said, you will know who they are, what kind of family they come from, and how they are the same or different from you.

Jewell Hembree is 12 and an only child in a two-parent family. Jewell enjoys rubber stamps and has more than 100 of them. Her favorite is a Winnie the Pooh stamp with her name on it. Jewell has lived in Colorado, Guam, Mississippi, and England. Her favorite place to live is Mississippi. Jewell enjoys listening to contemporary Christian music. Her favorite groups are dc Talk, Jars of Clay, Avalon, and Out of Eden. She also likes to read mystery and adventure books. Jewell and her family like to travel together.

Raul Stephenson is 12. He has a 13-year-old brother, Ricardo. Raul lives with his mom, brother, and his mom's cousin, Anna. His mom is from Spain and his dad grew up in Panama. Raul has lived in Italy, Washington D.C., Texas, Spain, and now lives in England. His parents are divorced and his dad lives in Puerto Rico. Raul likes playing computer strategy games, drawing, and rollerblading. Raul wants to be a lawyer like his cousins when he gets older.

Tyler Cassel is 8. He likes action figures, Legos, computer games, baseball, reading, and rollerblading. Tyler comes from a two-parent family but his family is unusual because he has a biological sister, Jessica, who is 7, and two adopted brothers, Jeff, age 5, and Adam, age 3. His family is made up of three different races. His brother Jeff is from Haiti and is African-American, and Adam is of mixed race. Tyler finds that people don't always believe he, Jeff, and Adam are brothers. Sometimes people treat his family differently because of all the different races of people in it. Tyler wants to be a Lego designer when he gets older.

Ashley Cassel is 15. She is a half sister to Tyler, but because they live with different sets of parents, they've only met three times. She lives with her mom, stepdad, and a 2-year-old half sister, Lydia. She has lived in both a group home for girls and a therapeutic foster home. Ashley likes to listen to CDs. Usher and Backstreet Boys are a couple of her favorite groups. Ashley is the only girl in her modern technology class at school. She collects posters, CDs, and pictures. She likes hanging out with her friends at the mall or going swimming or to the movies.

Micah Cleary is 11. He likes super heroes and reading comic books. He has 84 comic books in his collection. His favorites are "Green Lantern" and "Justice League of America." He also likes playing computer games. Micah is in Boy Scouts and likes to go camping. He is the oldest of three children in a two-parent family. Micah's younger brother, Steven, is 8, and his sister, Emily, is 5.

Matthew, David, and James Rettew are three of the 24 children in their family. Their family is made up of two biological children and 22 adopted children. There are 14 boys and 10 girls. Twenty-one of the children still live at home. The youngest is 15 months old and the oldest is 22 years old. Seven of them are teenagers. The children are of many different races and three are from countries other than the United States. Many of the children have special needs. All the children are homeschooled.

Matthew is 11 and has been part of the Rettew family since he was 3 days old. He sings with six of his siblings in churches, jails, nursing homes, and other places. He writes poetry and songs and would like to write a book. Matthew enjoys reading and likes *Adventures in Odyssey*. He enjoys playing soccer and football and likes living in a big family.

David, 12, is the spokesman for the seven siblings who sing together. He enjoys writing songs and poetry. He likes reading his Bible and wants to be a pastor when he gets older. David enjoys playing soccer and baseball. He collects shells when he goes to the beach once a month with his adopted dad. On Thanksgiving, David takes part in the Turkey Bowl soccer tournament his family has among themselves. David's favorite place to visit when they tour is Colorado because he likes the view and likes visiting Focus on the Family.

James is 14. He enjoys writing and would like to write a book about his family. James likes to read and is especially fond of history books. James collects coins and baseball cards. He likes to play soccer with his brothers. James is one of the siblings who sing together. He, along with Matthew and David, composed two of the songs the group sings. James likes being home-schooled and thinks it is good because your teachers are your parents and they know you best.

Josiah Tharp is 9. He lives with his two parents and brother, Aaron. Josiah is home-schooled. He does fifth- and sixth-grade work. Josiah likes nature. His family has a dog, a cat, two ferrets, fish, and a turtle. Josiah likes swimming, riding his bike, and playing with Legos. He is in Cub Scouts and a homeschool group. Josiah also likes planes and rockets, and isn't sure if he wants to design new Lego sets or be a missionary pilot when he gets older.

Aaron Tharp is 11. He lives with his two parents and brother, Josiah. Aaron is home-schooled and his favorite class is science. He is knowledgeable about insects, wild animals, and marine animals. He owns a ferret named Bandit and raised an abandoned Canadian goose last year. He is considering becoming a marine biologist when he gets older. Aaron is in Boy Scouts and a home-school group. He likes to play with Legos, study nature, and go camping.

Johnny Butler is 13. He lives with two parents. Johnny has an older brother, Albert, 17, an older sister, Esther, 15, and three younger sisters, Mary, 10, Tallie, 8, and Michaela, 7. Johnny has lived in Germany, New York, Hawaii, North Carolina, and now lives in England. Johnny likes baseball and playing Capture the Flag with his friends.

He plays Nintendo and computer games. Johnny collects crystal animals; his favorite is an eagle. Johnny went to Italy with Club Beyond, a youth evangelism program for military kids. He is on the student council at his junior high school.

Esther Butler is 15. She is the second oldest of six children, and the oldest girl. She takes on a lot of household responsibilities. Esther likes hanging out with friends and watching old black and white movies. She was one of the few girls on the wrestling team last year and was the junior high president. Esther collects photos of her friends. She plans to be a pediatrician in a country with children who need help. Esther babysits and works in her church nursery. Last summer she earned enough money from a summer job to buy her own TV/VCR combination. She also enjoys buying her own clothes.

As you can see from these examples, many different combinations of people can make up a family. You don't have to live in a two-parent family to have a fulfilling and happy life. In Christ, all families can have this! In the next chapter, we'll explore God's plan for families and how it leads to happiness and fulfillment.

HERE'S WHAT YOU SAID 📣

What is a family? Here's what some of you said:

" A family is like a team. Each person has a skill, and when you work together your team will get more points."
Micah Cleary, 11

"A family is people who are always there for you. You can always talk to them. They are like friends, but they're there all the time for you. I'm an only child so it's just me and my parents in my family." **Jewell Hembree, 12**

"People who love each other, take care of each other, and have fun together. Our family is different than most families because I have a biological sister and I have two adopted brothers who are different races than me."
Tyler Cassel, 8

"People who love each other and take care of each other. I live with just my mom, brother, and my mom's cousin since my dad left, but we are still a family."
Raul Stephenson, 12

"A family is like a team that works together to stay together and makes sure no one tears down the family. Our family is larger than most because there are 24 of us. Some of the kids have special needs and we all help with them." **Matthew Rettew, 11**

"A family is a group of siblings and parents who work together to understand each other. I think a family is important. Our family has more children than most and we go out and sing for Jesus. We adopted lots of children and we all love each other and try to understand each other." **James Rettew, 14**

"A group of people who live together and love each other and do things for each other. Families aren't all the same. Our family has six kids and most families only have two or three children."

Esther Butler, 15

"People you care about, love, and you would do just about anything for. No matter what you do, they still love you. All families aren't the same. I live with my mom, stepdad, and little sister, but I have four half brothers and sisters too. They are my family even though we don't live together."

Ashley Cassel, 15

"A family is a married couple of one man and one woman, with or without children. It could also include relatives living with them."

Aaron Tharp, 11

FOLLOWING THROUGH

Take a closer look at the people who make up your family unit. How is it the same or different from your friends' families?

Check all the people who make up your family:

___Dad   ___Uncle
___Mom   ___Grandmother
___Aunt   ___Grandfather
___Older sister(s) How many?_____
___Older brother(s)? How many?_____
___Twin/Triplets/other multiple births
___Younger sister(s) How many?_____
___Younger brother(s) How many?_____
___Foster children

How does your family differ from your friends' families? (people who make up your family, differences in activities and values, etc.)

_____

_____

_____

What does your family have in common with your friends' families? (same rules, similar activities, etc.)

_____

_____

_____

Write your own definition of family, based on your family:

_____

_____

_____

Why do you think God created families based on the verses for thought for this chapter?

_____

_____

_____

VERSES FOR THOUGHT

But for Adam no suitable helper was found. So the LORD God caused the man to fall into a deep sleep; and while he was sleeping, He took one of man's ribs and closed up the place with flesh. Then the LORD God made a woman from the rib He had taken out of the man, and He brought her to the man. The man said, "This is now bone of my bones and flesh of my flesh; she shall be called woman, for she was taken out of man." For this reason a man will leave his father and mother and be united to his wife, and they will become one flesh.

Genesis 2:20–24

He who finds a wife finds what is good and receives favor from the Lord.

Proverbs 18:22

Chapter 2

God's Plan for Families

Did God have a plan in mind when He created families? Yes! Starting in the Garden of Eden, the family was, and still is, the foundation of society. If we have strong families, we will have a strong society. In this chapter, we'll look at the importance of the family unit.

Kelly and Tara assembled their notes for their social studies project on the library table in front of them. They had been researching the role of families through the years.

"I interviewed my great-grandmother," Kelly said. "She said her parents had been disappointed they had three girls because they wanted boys to help run the farm. Gran said she and her sisters learned to pitch hay, milk a cow, and drive a truck before they were 10 years old!"

"I wish my parents would let me drive," Tara said.

"Gran was only allowed to drive on the farm. But she said in those days you could get a driver's license at 14 if you needed it to help your family," Kelly explained. "She said that her dad's brothers all lived on adjoining farms and got together for holidays, weddings, birthdays, and other celebrations. For funerals too."

"None of our relatives live near us," Tara said. "We move every three or four years because of Dad's job. It might be nice to have relatives close by. I have four cousins on my mom's side and nine on my dad's side, and I don't really know them. I see them about once every four years."

"I guess families have changed," Kelly said. "We don't have big celebrations like Gran talked about. Some of my relatives still live here but a lot of them live in different places around the United States and a couple even live in other countries. It's funny though, some things really haven't changed that much."

"Like what?" Tara asked.

"Gran talked about really wanting a transistor radio and getting told there were more important things to do with the money. That's almost the same thing my dad said when I asked for a CD player. I guess that's what Mr. Miller wanted us to learn—that in some ways families have changed but in other ways they are still the same."

Your Turn

Do you wonder why families exist? Did you ever stop to think what the world would be like if we didn't live in family units? Families are God's plan. Let's look at the beginning of families.

It Started in the Garden of Eden

When God created Adam, He formed him from the dust of the ground and put him to work caring for the garden. Then God said, "It is not good for man to be alone. I will make a helper suitable for him" (Genesis 2:18). God didn't want humans, His beloved creation, to go through life alone, so He created marriage. Genesis 2:24 says, "For this reason a man will leave his father and mother and be united to his wife, and they will become one flesh." From this one unit, the family is born.

God's Covenant with Noah

Do you remember the story of the flood in the Bible? (If not, read about it in Genesis 6:1–9:29.) After the flood, Noah and his family were the only people alive. Can you imagine a world with only your mom, dad, and siblings?

God told Noah's family, "As for you, be fruitful and increase in number; multiply on the earth and increase upon it" (Genesis 9:7). Part of God's plan for families was that they have children. In fact, children are a sign of God's favor. Psalm 127:5a says, "Blessed is the man whose quiver is full of [children]." Some married adults choose to have only one or two of these blessings; others choose to have many. Still others choose to have none. Some parents choose to bless their family by adopting children or raising foster children.

Families Through the Years

As Kelly discovered, families have changed. Years ago, "family" meant a man, his wife, and their children. Most families lived on farms and produced much of what they needed themselves. Whole families worked together. Extended family members, such as grandparents, often lived with the family as well. Families had to stick together through the hard times because they had no other choice.

Later, as factories opened, men went to work while their wives stayed home to take care of the children. Public schools opened for the first time. Children went to school and were no longer able to help as much at home.

After World War II, family life changed even more. Men returned home from the war ready to get married, buy homes, have children, and find jobs. Between 1946 and 1964 more than 72 million children were born. This was a time of growth and optimism. People wanted the "perfect" family with a husband, wife, and two or three children.

Since then, families have changed drastically. Women have careers and often wait until they are older to get married and have children. Many women return to work after having children and place their children in child care. Many people who aren't married are living together and having children. Unwed teenage girls are having babies. Some choose to parent their infants and others give their children up for adoption.

The divorce rate has been on the rise for many years. This means many children will live with a single parent or in a stepfamily if a parent remarries. A child may have two parents and two stepparents along with many step and half siblings.

Many things have changed, but one thing has not: The family is still the basic unit of society.

Has God's Plan Changed?

No. God's plan for families has not changed since the Garden of Eden. He still plans for one woman and one man to leave their parents and join together in marriage. He plans for them to raise their children together.

God also plans for different members of the family to have different roles. Ephesians 5:1–6:4 talks about the roles of the husband, wife, and children. To the husband, God says, "Husbands, love your wives, just as Christ loved the church and gave Himself up for her" (Ephesians 5:25). Christ loved us enough to be willing to die for us. That's the kind of love God plans for a husband to have for his wife.

To the wife, God says, "Wives, submit to your husbands as to the Lord" (Ephesians 5:22). Just as Christ is the head of the church, the husband is the head of the home. This means that just as you trust Christ does what is best for you, a wife will trust and respect her husband to do what's right for his family.

God's words to children are, "Children, obey your parents in the Lord, for this is right" (Ephesians 6:1). This may not be easy to do all the time, but it's part of God's plan for the family. The only way families will be truly happy is by doing things God's way. But families aren't alone as they try to live according to God's plan. God will always provide strength and patience as they live and grow together, Christ's love working in the heart of each family member will help families love each other, and His grace will cover all the times family members fail to live by God's plan.

HERE'S WHAT YOU SAID

Why do you think God created the family unit? Here's what some of you said:

"So we could have people to love, to care for, and to live with. Families are for loving." **Tyler Cassel, 8**

"To have people to live with and take care of you and provide for you. They provide love, keep you safe, and want you to be healthy." **Raul Stephenson, 12**

"I believe it was so people could reproduce. It also makes sense to me that God created the family so they could help each other out. I also think He didn't want people to be alone." **Josiah Tharp, 9**

"So that we can love each other and help each other out with problems."   Micah Cleary, 11

"I think God made families so people wouldn't be lonely. He doesn't want people to be alone." Jewell Hembree, 12

"So you can have people to love you and take care of you when you can't do it yourself." Ashley Cassel, 15

"So we could have people to talk to and take care of us when we can't do it for ourselves. We can be a family to those who need one." Matthew Rettew, 11

"A family is good to have. We need a mom and dad to love us and show us the way to go. We can learn more about God from them." David Rettew, 12

"God put us in families because He knew we would do better in families and to have someone to talk to and to help us know Jesus." James Rettew, 14

FOLLOWING THROUGH

Ask a grandparent or older relative to tell you about family life when he or she were young. What responsibilities did he or she have? How were holidays celebrated? What did he or she do for fun? During summer vacation? How did his or her family life differ from yours today?

_____

_____

_____

Do you watch any TV shows that portray families? How does their portrayal of family life differ from your family life?

_____

_____

_____

Do most families you see on TV follow God's plan for families? Why or why not?

_____

_____

What does God say is your responsibility in the family? How can you do this better? Who will help you?

_____

_____

_____

Verses for Thought

A father to the fatherless, a defender of widows, is God in His holy dwelling. God sets the lonely in families, He leads forth the prisoners with singing.

Psalm 68:5–6a

He who began a good work in you will carry it on to completion until the day of Christ Jesus.

Philippians 1:6

CHAPTER 3

Nontraditional Families

We talked in the first chapter about the definition of a family. A family isn't always a mother, a father, and two children. In this chapter, we'll look at some nontraditional families, their challenges, and their advantages.

Brendon dribbled the basketball, jumped up, and let the ball fly toward the hoop. Two points. He ran to his position to guard his opponent. Brendon avoided glancing toward the bleachers where his parents were. He knew he should be thankful that both of them had come to his game, but he was embarrassed too. Seeing his mom sit at one end of the bleachers and his dad at the other end was a reminder to him, as well as to all his friends, that his parents weren't together anymore.

After the game Brendon walked over to his dad to say a hurried good-bye.

"Thanks for coming," he said.

"Are you coming over this weekend?" his dad asked.

"Yeah, I guess so. Michelle is having a slumber party and I don't want to be there for that," Brendon said. "See ya."

Brendon hurried to catch up with his teammates who were headed to the locker room. He remembered two years earlier when his whole family had gone to sporting events together. Brendon had no idea his parents were having problems until his dad told Brendon he was moving out. Brendon had wanted to live with his dad but both his parents agreed it was better for him and his two younger sisters to live with his mom.

Now his dad was dating a woman with two young daughters and Brendon feared that not only would he have two sisters, he'd also have two stepsisters. Ugh!

YOUR TURN

Everyone is discontent with their family some time during their life. Physical and emotional changes during junior high and high school can put added stress on family relationships. If you are in a nontraditional family, this complicates things even more. But it doesn't have to mean an unhappy family life or problems within your family. When everyone works together, family life can be fun— even beneficial.

Single Parent Families

Half the youth today will live in a single-parent family at some time in their lives. Most single-parent families are a result of separation or divorce, but sometimes they form when one parent dies. Single-parent families are also formed when an unmarried mother raises a child, when one parent goes to jail, or when a parent needs long-term medical or psychological care. Sometimes single people choose to adopt and become single parents.

One of the biggest problems for single-parent families is a lack of money. Supporting a family on one income puts a strain on the budget. If you are in a one-parent family you may have had to give up some things such as extra spending money or music lessons.

Your parent may also have to work long hours and you may have extra responsibilities around the house. By the time your parent comes home from work, he or she may be very tired and not feel like cooking or checking your homework.

When problems occur, talk with your parent about your feelings. Be respectful, but also be honest. Hiding your feelings doesn't help anyone. You may be able to solve some problems easily, others may take compromise.

Being in a single-parent family may mean more after-school responsibilities, but it also means learning to be responsible and independent earlier. You learn to make decisions about meals and activities. You learn what it takes to run a house. This will help you if you become a baby-sitter or when you have your own family.

Mixed Race Families

Mixed race families happen when the parents are different races or when the family adopts children of a different race. A big problem for these families is prejudice. People judge the family by skin color. Since not everyone in the family has the same color skin, some people think it is not a "normal" family.

If you are in a mixed race family, you may have had unkind things said to you by other people, even kids in your own school. You may feel hurt or angry. When this happens, talk to a parent, teacher, school counselor, or pastor about your feelings. They will help you understand the situation, and deal with the people involved.

Whatever race, or mix of races, you are, find out more about your heritage. What famous people are of your race? What is your history? In what cultural activities does your race participate? Find out as much as you can. You can create a special scrapbook for this project. Be proud of your heritage.

Stepfamilies

Stepfamilies are formed when two adults, one or both of whom have children, marry. Sometimes all the children live together.

When two separate families join together to form a stepfamily, it means changes for everyone. You may have to move to a new home, decide what to call your new step-parent, and adjust to new siblings.

Sometimes things go well and the new stepfamily adjusts easily to one another. Other times fighting and bad feelings can happen. It helps if everyone can sit down and talk about the problems. If this is hard to do, a family counselor or pastor can be helpful.

Being in a stepfamily means having additional relatives. You may gain another set of grandparents, aunts, uncles, and cousins. You may find they have holiday traditions and family celebrations you enjoy. You can blend some of your family traditions to make new ones or keep the best traditions from both families.

Adoptive Families

Many types of adoption are available to families. Parents can choose private infant adoption and agency infant adoptions. In this case, the adoptive parents may meet the birth mother or write to her if this is what everyone wants. Older children and hard-to-place children—those who have a handicap or are past the cute age—can be adopted through both private and state agencies as well. Sometimes these children are adopted in sibling groups. Children of all ages are being adopted from countries throughout the world. The countries which allow their children to be adopted change. At this time, many families adopt children from China or Eastern Europe.

People don't always adopt because they can't have bio-logical children. Some adults adopt because that is how they want to form their family. Other families have both biological and adopted children.

If you are adopted, you may know a lot about your birth parents, or you may know nothing about them. Maybe you wonder what your life would have been like if your biological mom was raising you. At some point you may struggle with the fact that your biological parents chose not to raise you; at other times you may be thankful for the life your adoptive parents have given you. You may find that your feelings about adoption change as you get older. It may help if you and your family join an adoption support group to talk about your feelings and to meet other adoptive families.

Your parents may be keeping a special book for you with your adoption story and photos. If they aren't, you can make one yourself. Include information about how your parents applied to adopt, when they first heard about you, and how and when you joined the family. Have copies made of important photographs and include them in your book. It will help give you a sense of who you are.

Foster Families

Foster parents are people who take care of children who are not their biological or adopted children. They go to training sessions to learn how to handle the problems and challenges of being foster parents, such as helping children who have been abused or helping children who have special medical needs. Social workers visit foster homes to make sure there is enough room for everyone to sleep, study, and live.

Children enter foster care because their parents are unable to care for them. The parents may be abusive or addicted to drugs or alcohol, or they may not know how to take care of children. Sometimes the parents may just be too ill to take care of their children.

Sometimes foster children become available for adoption. Other times they are returned home once the problems are solved. A few children, especially those who enter foster care when they are older, live in foster care until they are old enough to be on their own.

If you are in foster care, you may have some bad feelings about it. You may blame your parents or your foster parents for your feelings. Talking to a school counselor or pastor about your feelings may help, or perhaps there is a support group you can join. When you are part of a support group, you realize that you are not alone in your feelings.

If you are in a good foster home, you may learn many things you wouldn't learn in your own home. You might learn new hobbies or sports, how to live as part of a family, and how to handle problems. This will help you when you return to your own home or when you have your own family.

Families Headed by Other Relatives

Grandparents, aunts, and uncles or other relatives may be called on to raise children. Some children have been raised by relatives for so long it is the only home they have known. Others go to live with relatives later and remember living with their own parents.

As in any kind of family, change can lead to stress if the family doesn't talk about the problems and compromise on solutions. If your family can't work through the problems themselves, often a pastor, counselor, or therapist can help. Or you can talk to a school counselor or pastor by yourself. Good family relationships take lots of hard work. And you know what? The work is worth it because everything you are learning about family living now will help you later when you are the parent.

God Knows Your Family

One thing remains the same no matter what kind of family you are a part of: God knows all about your family. He knows the problems, the stress points, the positive side—everything. And He cares. He cares about you and your family. God, our Heavenly Father, created the family and He wants it to be a place where you can learn and grow and be loved.

God gives us another type of family too—our family in Christ. Because humans are sinful, there's no way we could ever be perfect, or have a perfect family life. But Christ died on the cross to forgive our imperfections, and rose from the dead so that one day we all may live in Heaven with Him and the rest of our Christian family. Until then, our Christian family will support us and our real families, give us encouragement and love, and guide us as we learn more about Jesus.

HERE'S WHAT YOU SAID

Are adoptive, foster, step, and mixed race families the same as or different from the traditional two-parent family? Here's what some of you said:

"Adoptive families are different but just as good. I have

one biological sister and two adopted brothers. We can still love each other but we aren't all born from the same parents. I think it's good to adopt kids who need homes. That's what we did. I want an adopted sister too."

Tyler Cassel, 8

"Single-parent families aren't the same. My dad is far away and I have to write to him instead of see him. I have to mow the lawn and do other jobs he did. I didn't get to play baseball because my mom works late and my dad wasn't there to take me. I have to be by myself until my mom gets home from work."

Raul Stephenson, 12

"It's harder living in a stepfamily because one parent isn't your real parent. I don't really respect my stepdad because I don't care as much about him as my real dad. But I don't get to see my real dad very often, only every two or three years. You don't always get to know your half siblings if they don't live with you. I haven't even met one of my brothers and one of them I only saw once when he was a baby. I want to be with my half siblings while they grow up. I want them to know me and I want them to know they can count on me if they need me. I have friends but it isn't the same as brothers and sisters.

I also have lived in a group home for girls and in a foster home. In the group home I was the youngest and the other girls treated me like a little sister, helping me with my homework and stuff like that. They were just regular teens who were having a rough time and couldn't live at home. I liked it better than the foster home I was in because in the foster home they didn't treat me like I was part of the family. I was there the whole school year and I didn't like it. They took me to a concert and bought me a T-shirt but when I went back to live with my mom they kept the shirt. I was glad to get things worked out and go to counseling with my mom so I could move back home."

Ashley Cassel, 15

"I think it would be harder to live in a single-parent family because the parent would have to work and there would be no one there in the house for the kids. I don't think it would be harder to live in a mixed race family because color does not make a difference. Adopting a child, if you are capable of doing so, would be a lot harder. Having someone new in your family would mean that you have to give up certain things like a room by yourself. I think it would be worth it though."   Aaron Tharp, 11

"I think it would be harder to live in a single-parent family because you would have only one parent to take care of you instead of two. It might be a little bit harder to be in a mixed race family because some people might be prejudiced against your family. I don't think it would be harder to be in an adoptive family because if you adopt someone, you must want them in your family. It might be hard getting used to someone new in the house, but I think I would like it."   Josiah Tharp, 9

"We adopt for the Lord. We are just doing what the Lord wants us to do. We pray before we take in a new child. Adoptive families are special and they can care for kids who need care."   Matthew Rettew, 11

"It's about the same living in an adoptive family. We do the same things kids in other families do—play and talk. We have a lot of kids and we take in special needs kids but we're really no different than other families."

David Rettew, 12

"Some people may think our family is different because we are adoptive and we are different colors and some of the kids have special needs, but God made us all equal and He knew we all needed families. Color and special needs don't matter; we just have to be more careful of those that have special needs and give them extra help."

James Rettew, 14

FOLLOWING THROUGH

Is your family like one of the families we talked about in this chapter? What kind of family do you have?

_____

_____

_____

What kind of families do your best friends live in? How are those families different from your own family?

_____

_____

_____

In this chapter we looked at some advantages and disadvantages of each kind of family. What advantages and disadvantages does your family have?

_____

_____

_____

Do you believe that God knows all about your family and has a plan especially for you? Read the verses for thought to see what God says to you. Write down your thoughts.

_____

_____

_____

VERSES FOR THOUGHT

The LORD watches over the alien and sustains the fatherless and the widows.

Psalm 146:9a

"For I know the plans I have for you," declares the LORD, "plans to prosper you and not to harm you, plans to give you hope and a future. Then you will call upon Me and come and pray to Me, and I will listen to you. You will seek Me and find Me when you seek Me with all your heart."

Jeremiah 29:11–13

Chapter 4

Eight Things Every Family Needs

Even though all families are different, happy families share some of the same characteristics. In this chapter, we'll look at eight characteristics of happy families mentioned most often by parents and teens.

Erin walked home from school with her friend Amy. She looked forward to the evening they would spend at Amy's house. As they walked through the door, the smell of cooking food greeted them.

"It's about a half hour until supper if you girls have homework to do," Amy's mom told them.

"Okay, we'll get done as quickly as we can," Amy said, giving her mom a quick kiss as they went by her on the way to Amy's room.

Erin and Amy dropped their book bags and got out their math homework. Erin looked around the room Amy shared with two younger sisters. Bunk beds and a twin bed crowded the room. The carpet was worn and Amy's desk has been bought at a secondhand store and refinished. Erin had helped Amy and her dad sand and varnish it.

Erin could hear Amy's two brothers laughing in the next bedroom. "Why is it that I feel so at home here?" Erin asked herself. "I have my own room, a new bed and desk, and even the latest computer with Internet access. Why is it that I would rather be here with Amy than at my own home?"

Erin tried to concentrate on her math, but she couldn't shake the feeling that her family was missing out on something that Amy's family had.

Your Turn

Can you think of some characteristics your family has? Which ones make your family a happy family? If you can't think of any, maybe you'll get some ideas from what other families said. Let's look at eight characteristics shared by most happy families.

Eight Characteristics of a Happy Family

I asked children, teens, and parents to list what characteristics they thought a happy family had. Some characteristics appeared on many lists. Sometimes people used different words to describe the same characteristic. Following are the ideas most commonly mentioned.

Love Families who love God and love one another are the happiest families. Most families I spoke to listed love as the most important characteristic because when family members really love one another, they are willing to work at problem areas and accept and support one another. Here are some characteristics of love listed in 1 Corinthians 13 that you can put into practice into your family.

- Love is patient.
- Love is kind.
- Love does not envy.
- Love does not boast.
- Love is not proud.
- Love is not rude.
- Love is not self-seeking.
- Love is not easily angered.
- Love keeps no record of wrong.
- Love does not delight in evil.

- Love rejoices with truth.
- Love always protects.
- Love always trusts.
- Love always hopes.
- Love always perseveres.
- Love never fails.

Communication Families who take time to talk will know what is going on in one another's lives. Talking lets families share ideas, encouragement, and suggestions. It lets them offer one another support. Most of the families I interviewed feel communication is very important, but many of them think they need to work on this area. If you need help with communication, be sure to read chapter 8, in which we look at communication more in-depth. For now, here are a few ideas for talking with your parents:

- Each day share with your parents one thing that happened at school.
- Each day ask your parents one question about their day, such as what was the best or worst thing that happened or the most fun thing they did.
- Share an important idea or decision with your parents.
- Ask your parents for advice when you have problems. Don't rely only on friends for advice.
- Talk to your parents about really important things, such as God, dating, and your future.

Teamwork If you've ever played on a sports team, were in the cast or crew of a play, or belonged to a musical group, you know the importance of teamwork. You know it takes everyone working together to produce good results. The same is true for families. Each family member, whether parent or child, has something important and unique to contribute to the happiness and strength of the family. When everyone works together, problems can be addressed and solutions can be found. Many families I talked to also feel it is important to work together to help any family member who has a problem or needs extra help in some area. Here are some ideas they shared about teamwork:

- Be honest about family problems.
- Be willing to talk about problems.
- Find a way for everyone to help or be part of the solution.
- Look for projects to do together that involve all family members.
- Look for family projects that can be enjoyed by everyone.
- Cheer for one another whether you're winning or losing.

Acceptance No one is perfect; we are all sinful, flawed human beings. This is why God sent His Son, Jesus, to die on the cross to forgive our sins. Through Jesus, we are made perfect and acceptable to God. When Christ is part of our family, we can be accepted there as well. His love and grace helps to make families a place of safety where no one is ridiculed for having a physical, mental, or other imperfection. Name calling and making fun of each other tears down a family; acceptance builds it up. Families interviewed for this book almost always listed acceptance as one of the most important characteristics, but many of the teens said they didn't always feel accepted. They also said they had problems accepting their siblings. Many had good ideas for improving in this area, including:

- Talking about differences.
- Sharing ideas and feelings.
- Being respectful of one another's feelings.
- Being respectful of one another's right to be different.
- Looking for similarities in ideas, values, and interests.
- Setting boundaries and rules that work for everyone.

Empathy Empathy is more than just sympathy. Sympathy is feeling bad for someone, but empathy is understanding and caring how another person feels. Caring and supporting one another builds a family up. How can you show you care? Here are some ideas:

- When a family member looks depressed or upset, ask what is wrong.
- Take time to listen when a family member is upset.
- Offer to help when you can. Care about the problem even when you can't help.
- Pray for or with a family member who has a problem.
- Care about other people's problems even if they seem trivial to you.

Common goals Having common goals makes it easier to work together as a team. It also gives you a common purpose that will help you unite together. One goal of every Christian family should be to live in a way that honors God. Families share other goals also. What those goals are depends on the members within the family. Here are some real-life family goals:

- To help each family member find his or her special talents and develop them.
- For each family member to receive a good education.
- To make family fitness a priority.

- To read the Bible together each day.
- To take part in summer missions as a family.
- To set aside time for fun.

Respect Respect means thinking someone has value, in God's eyes and in yours. Respect isn't just something due adults. Everyone in your family deserves respect, including you. You may not like everything your parents and siblings do, but you can respect their rights and their feelings. How can you do that? Here are some ideas:

- Listen when other family members talk. Let them share their feelings.
- Don't criticize or ridicule another family member's feelings. Accept his or her feelings even if you don't agree.
- Don't bring up family problems outside the family.
- Ask before borrowing anyone else's belongings.
- Return what you borrow.
- Treat your parents' and siblings' belongings as you want them to treat yours.
- Treat the other members of your family as you want them to treat you. (See Matthew 7:12.)

Shared interests Families can share a variety of interests from mountain climbing to working jigsaw puzzles to shooting archery. The time spent together developing skills and hobbies is time that unites and bonds family members. Here are some hobbies shared by the families who helped with this book:

- Roller-skating and ice-skating.
- Running, walking.
- Archery.

- Working jigsaw puzzles.
- Camping, cooking out.
- Going to amusement parks.
- Going to the lake.
- Eating out at new restaurants.
- Swimming and skiing.
- Going to the zoo.
- Hiking.
- Working in a rescue mission.

HERE'S WHAT YOU SAID

What one thing is most important for a family to have in order to be happy? Here's what some of you said:

"The Lord in their lives. The Lord shows love to parents so they can love us and we can pass it down to our families when we have them later." **David Rettew, 12**

"The most important thing families can do is to help each other and not to tear each other down." **James Rettew, 14**

"Love. A family wouldn't have fun together if they didn't love each other." **Tyler Cassel, 8**

"Basically they just need to love each other." **Micah Cleary, 11**

"Space. I need my own space away from my brother. We have to share a room and computer. Also respect because if you don't respect your family they won't respect you." **Raul Stephenson, 12**

"To be truly happy they have to be Christians because you can't truly be happy without the Lord. They also need to love each other and God gives them love for each other."
Jewell Hembree, 12

"Respect. You have to have that to get along together."
Esther Butler, 15

"Love. Without love a family doesn't work."
Johnny Butler, 13

"Love and togetherness. They go hand in hand. You can't really love someone if you aren't close to them and if you love them you will be close to them. Families need both."
Ashley Cassel, 15

FOLLOWING THROUGH

Look at the list of eight characteristics mentioned in the chapter:

__Love	__Empathy
__Communication	__Common goals
__Teamwork	__Respect
__Acceptance	__Shared interests
_____	_____

Number these items from 1–8 according to how important you think each one is. Number 1 should be the most important and number 8 the least important. There are two blank places for you to add other characteristics you think are important.

Which characteristic did you choose as most important? Why?

_____

_____

_____

_____

Now reread the list and put a + by those characteristics you personally demonstrate in your home. Put a 0 by those you sometimes demonstrate and a - by those you need to work on.

Choose one characteristic to demonstrate in your family this week. Which one do you choose and how can you put it into practice?

_____

_____

_____

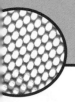

VERSES FOR THOUGHT

Trust in the LORD with all your heart and lean not on your own understanding; in all your ways acknowledge Him, and He will make your paths straight.

Proverbs 3:5–6

But the fruit of the Spirit is love, joy, peace, patience, kindness, goodness, faithfulness, gentleness and self-control. Against such things there is no law.

Galatians 5:22–23

Parents

Chapter 5

God's Plan for Parents

Parents! Sometimes they can be really hard to understand. They say they love you, but they yell at you when you come home late, make you eat food you detest, and embarrass you in front of your friends. Are parents really necessary? Yes, they are necessary—in fact, parents were God's idea!

Devon slunk up the school steps. He dreaded facing Tyrill and Mitch. How could he tell them he couldn't go to the concert after all?

"Hey, Devon," Tyrill greeted him as he entered the school. "So, what's the answer? Are you going with us Saturday night?"

"Nah, my stepdad nixed that."

"Why? It's going to be great!" Mitch said. "You're going to be the only one not going."

"Yeah, don't rub it in. It's bad enough already. My stepdad went and bought one of the band's CDs and listened to it. He went over the lyrics and highlighted all the things 'against our value system.' Can you believe it?"

"What do you mean 'against your value system?'

"Tyrill asked.

"Some of the songs were about living together before marriage, getting drunk, and things like that. My stepdad says he can't let me fill my mind with that kind of stuff because he loves me. Well, if he loved me he'd let me

go to this concert, that's what he'd do."

"I don't know," Mitch said. "Sometimes I wish my dad would pay attention to anything I did. I don't think he even knows where I go or what I listen to."

"Yeah, well, I wish my stepdad didn't pay so much attention," Devon said. "Sometimes I just want to do my own thing."

Your Turn

Is your family like Devon's, or Mitch's family? Do you wonder why you really need parents? Well, believe it or not, parents are important to you. God has given them the responsibility to care for you. Let's look at some of the things parents are supposed to do.

What's Their Job?

It would be hard to write a job description for parents. Parents begin their role when the first child joins the family, or even before that when they first learn they are going to be parents and begin preparing for their new role. Becoming a parent usually means night feedings, diaper changes, and a lack of sleep. The parental role changes somewhat as the child matures. Midnight feedings are replaced by chaperoning field trips and packing lunches, teaching children how to pump their legs on the playground swing, and putting Band-Aids on cuts and scrapes.

By now your parents are probably responsible for driving you to baseball practice or piano lessons, signing permission slips, providing lunch money, helping with difficult homework, and teaching you how to do many things for yourself.

The Many Roles of Parents

No matter how old you are, some basic parental roles don't change. Here are a few of them:

Disciplinarian Your parents are in charge of making fair rules and setting boundaries for you. When you were little you probably had boundaries and rules such as not crossing the street without help, not going into a friend's house without asking permission, and coming straight home from school. These rules and boundaries have changed to reflect your growing independence, but the rules you are given now are still just as important as the ones you had when you were younger.

Of course, just as when you were younger, if you break a rule you receive a consequence. You are past the days of spankings or time out, but your parents still enforce the rules by punishing you for breaking them. The punishments may be loss of television or computer privileges, grounding, or missing special events. While these might sometimes seem unfair, they are necessary.

The book of Hebrews compares God's discipline with an earthly father's discipline. It says:

> Endure hardship as discipline; God is treating you as sons. For what son is not disciplined by his father? If you are not disciplined (and everyone undergoes discipline), then you are illegitimate children and not true sons. Moreover we have all had human fathers who disciplined us and we respected them for it. How much more should we submit to the Father of our spirits and live! Our fathers disciplined us for a little while as they thought best; but God disciplines us for our

good, that we may share in His holiness. No discipline seems pleasant at the time, but painful. Later on, however, it produces a harvest of righteousness and peace for those who have been trained by it.

Hebrews 12:7–11

Parental discipline, as well as God's discipline, is necessary to lead you in the right direction. In the long run, it will help you live a good and peaceful life.

Provider Think of all the things you need—school supplies, clothes, food, activity money, school lunch money. Then add things you want like CDs, specialty clothing, team registration money, lesson money, fast food money, and so on. All that money adds up. Try sitting down and making a list of all the money your parents spend on you in a month. Ask them to check your list. You may be surprised at how much money they spend on you!

If you want more clothes, CDs, movies, and fast food than they are willing to provide, talk to them about ways to earn your own money. Have them help you set up a budget for your money. Along with being your providers, your parents can help you learn to be financially responsible now, so you avoid serious mistakes when you are an adult and are providing for yourself or your own family.

Example Young children especially learn by watching those around them. When you were little, you watched the important people in your life and tried to do the things they did. Your parents were your first and your most important role models. You learned to talk by copying them and learned to walk by copying them. You probably picked up some of their habits such as wiping your feet before entering a room, putting the remote controls in a certain place, or folding over the potato chip bag.

Now you can learn important values and life lessons by observing your parents. You can learn how to deal with someone who is angry, how to budget money, how to relate to an employer, how to admit to mistakes, how to patch up a friendship, how to get along with people who are different than you are, and many other things.

Sometimes special problems such as alcoholism or abuse can keep parents from being the examples they should be. In this case someone such as a teacher, youth leader, or a friend's parents may be your example.

Nurturer A nurturing parent lets you know how much you are loved and how important you are to the family. When you were an infant, your parents nurtured you by rocking you and holding you close. Now they may do it by saying, "I'm proud of you" or giving you a pat on the back or buying you a special reward.

Is this really important? Yes! Orphanage workers found that infants who weren't held and nurtured would die—that's how important it is. It's still important as we get older. No, you won't die if no one nurtures you now, but you can end up feeling unloved and unwanted. So next time your mom tries to hug you, let her—and hug her back!

Guidance counselor This role never ends. It started with those problems of how to handle the neighborhood bully or how to make friends with the new neighbor. Now your parents may offer advice about what classes to take in school, how to handle problems with your teachers, and what to do to mend friendships.

Most parents are willing to help you and offer advice even long after you have moved away from home. You may not always agree with their advice, but listen to it, pray about it, and with God's help, make the best decisions you can.

Faith nurturer Helping children grow in their faith is one of the most important jobs of parents. This has been true since Bible times. For instance, the children of Israel got to witness firsthand the miracles and provisions of the Lord. But they didn't tell their children and grandchildren about these things. Judges 2:10 tells us, "After that whole generation had been gathered to their fathers, another generation grew up, who knew neither the Lord nor what He had done for Israel."

In contrast to the Children of Israel, Timothy—another Bible figure—was raised by his mother and grandmother to be sincere in his faith. "I have been reminded of your sincere faith, which first lived in your grandmother Lois and in your mother Eunice and, I am persuaded, now lives in you also" (2 Timothy 1:5). Timothy knew the scriptures from his very youngest days (2 Timothy 3:15). His mother and grandmother fulfilled the role of passing on the faith.

When your parents take you to church and special youth activities, share Scripture with you, pray with you, or share information about their Christian walk with you, they are living as examples of their faith. By doing so, they help you to grow in your faith, and they teach you how to set an example to others.

HERE'S WHAT YOU SAID

What is the most important job of a parent? Here's what some of you said:

"Their role is to love, mentor, and protect their children."
Micah Cleary, 11

"To train us on how to live our lives and become an adult. To bring us up the best way possible."   Esther Butler, 15

"To teach us about God. By teaching us about God they are preparing us for how to live our lives the best way."
Jewell Hembree, 12

"The most important job of parents is to help us know Jesus. If they do their best they can look back and have the assurance that they raised us to know about Jesus."
James Rettew, 14

"To provide and look after us. They go to work to get money to provide food and keep a roof over us. They get us things we need like school supplies and clothes."
Raul Stephenson, 12

"To get us ready for life, to get us ready to be an adult."
Johnny Butler, 13

"To teach us the things we need to know. To be an example for us."   Ashley Cassel, 15

"To love and teach their children about God. A parent's role is also to help their children grow by teaching them about discipline, love, and character."   Aaron Tharp, 11

Following Through

What roles do each of your parents assume?

_____

_____

_____

How do they assume the role of disciplinarian? What punishments do they use? Have you talked with them about it?

_____

_____

_____

What things have your parents provided for you this week? Do they give you an allowance or opportunity to earn extra money?

_____

_____

How important is it for parents to set the example for their children? What can you do if the example they set isn't a positive one?

_____

_____

_____

Can you think of examples of how your parents nurture you? If not, you may want to discuss this with them.

_____

_____

_____

How important do you think it is to listen to parental advice? (Check out Proverbs 1:8–9 to see what Solomon says about it.)

_____

_____

_____

In what ways are your parents passing on their faith to you?

_____

_____

_____

Read the James passage in "Verses for Thought."

How are your parents gifts to you from God?

_____

_____

_____

VERSES FOR THOUGHT

We will tell the next generation the praiseworthy deeds of the LORD, His power, and the wonders He has done. ... Then they would put their trust in God and would not forget His deeds but would keep His commands.

Psalm 78:4, 7

Every good and perfect gift is from above, coming down from the Father of the heavenly lights, who does not change like shifting shadows. He chose to give us birth through the word of truth, that we might be a kind of first-fruits of all He created.

James 1:17–18

Chapter 6

Understanding Your Parents

What really makes your parents tick—and ticked? Why do they do what they do? What do parents really want anyway? Have you ever asked yourself these questions? Believe it or not, your parents may have asked the same questions when they were your age.

Michaela threw her book bag to the floor. She dropped to her bed before asking her friend Aimee, "How can I win with my mom? I'm either too old to do something or too young to do something!"

"I have the same problem," Aimee admitted. "I will never understand my parents. If I start goofing around or trying to have fun, they say, 'You're too old to act like that.' But if I ask to go to the mall on the weekend it's, 'You're too young to be there by yourself.'"

Michaela sighed. "Yesterday Kayleigh made me really mad and I threw my socks at her—like that's really going to hurt her—and Mom said, 'You're too old to act like that,' but nothing happens to Kayleigh. I think my mom's forgotten what it's like to be a kid."

"Mine too. I bet my parents did some of the same things that they yell at me for doing. They just don't remember what it's like anymore. Sometimes I wish parents came with an owner's guide so we could understand them."

"Or program them," Michaela said, laughing.

Your Turn

Do you wish you had some kind of manual or guide to help you figure out what makes your parents do the things they do? Or, maybe like Michaela, you wish you could program them like you do a VCR. The ability to program them isn't likely to happen, but you can learn to understand your parents better. In this chapter you'll find ideas to get you started.

Looking Back

If you look ahead to the "Here's What You Said" section, you'll notice most of the youth thought how their parents were raised or what kind of families they came from made their parents who they are today. This is partly true. Much of what happens while we are growing up makes us who we are, including when and where we grow up and what kind of family we come from. In this section, we'll look at these things and give you some questions to ask yourself or discuss with your parents. The answers to the questions will help you get to know your parents better.

When Did Your Parents Grow Up? The time period in which a person grows up makes a difference. My dad was born in the early part of the 1900s, so he lived through the depression. The economy was poor and his family was poor. Times were tough. When he and his siblings were young, they were expected to get jobs working in gardens or doing chores for neighbors. Because their family needed money to live, it was more important for the children to work than go to school. Knowing all of this about my dad—what life was like as he grew up—helped me partly understand why he did some of the things he did. For instance, I didn't ask for many new clothes, but one time I wanted two new dresses for senior photos. He made sure I got them. He said he remembered what it felt like not to be able to get anything new and he wanted me to be able to get new clothes when it was really important.

Knowing what life was like when your parents grew up will also give you some insights into who they are now. Ask your parents the following questions.

- What was going on in the world when your parents were born? (Wars, politics, etc.)
- How did this affect their families? (Was an older sibling in the Vietnam war or did both parents need to work?)
- What was the economy like?
- What kind of jobs did their parents have?
- What music, movies, and clothing were popular?
- What were schools like?

Think about the answers to these questions. Discuss them with your parents. Can you see how these things may have influenced who your parents are today? Do you think your parents would be different from who they are if these circumstances had been different?

What Kind of Family Did Your Parents Come from? Most of the people I talked to thought this was one of the most important factors that influence people. They felt how their parents were raised made them the people they are today. Why? Parental influence is very strong. For instance, sometimes when people come from an alcoholic or abusive family, they end up drinking or hitting their spouse or kids—even if they've said they never would. They haven't had any other role model from which to learn. Positive family traits are also passed down, such as being a good listener, encourager, or nurturer.

One friend shared how her parents included the children when they made big decisions. They would discuss the situation and possible solutions. Then they would listen to each child talk about how he or she felt and what he or she wanted. For instance, one time the family was going to move. There was no choice because the father was being transferred to another part of the country. However, the family looked at several houses they could buy. Before the parents made a final choice, they had a family meeting to hear which house each of the children liked best and why. Then they made the best choice for everyone.

Now this person does the same thing with her family. When there is a major decision to make, all the children get to have a say in it.

Other influential factors in your parents' lives may be how they were disciplined, how openly affection was shown, whether or not they had siblings, how many siblings they had, and how much responsibility they had at home. Look at the list of questions below. Try to answer them. Discuss them with your parents.

- What are your grandparents like? (Loud, quiet, openly affectionate, strict, lenient, etc.)

- What were they like when your parents were growing up?

- How many siblings did your parents have?

- Were your parents the youngest, oldest, or the middle children?

- What responsibilities did your parents have? (Babysitting siblings, house work, farm work, part-time job, etc.)

- What activities were they involved in? (School,

church, family activities)

All of these family characteristics play a part in who your parents are today. In the same way, the things you are doing right now will affect your parenting when that time comes. You may find yourself saying things your mother said to you. You might even find yourself doing things you say now you will never do.

Today

What Is Important to Your Parents Now? Most families have things which are important to them. Sometimes families take time to think about what is most important and what they really want to accomplish as a family. They may even write a mission statement to help them focus on what is important to them.

Our family mission statement is, "To provide an atmosphere of love and acceptance where each person is encouraged to develop his or her unique talents and characteristics." This helps us focus on what is really important—accepting each person as God made him or her, encouraging each person to be his or her best, and to discover and develop the talents God has given each person. This may not be as important to other families.

Even if a family doesn't sit down and write a mission statement, they may still have strong priorities that influence who they are and how they live. Asking yourself some questions may help you focus on what is most important to your parents. Read the questions below. Discuss them with your parents.

- What are the top priorities for your parents? (Getting ahead in their jobs, saving for the future, spending fun time as a family, serving God as a family, etc.)

- What do they spend the most time and money on?

- What values are most important to them? (Honesty, hard work, integrity, kindness, etc.)

- What goals do they have for your family?

All the things above determine who your parents are and what they do. The more you know about your parents' goals and priorities, the better you will understand them. If you don't know the answers to some of these questions, you may want to ask your parents and really listen to their answers.

Here are some other questions to think about:

- What are your parents' daily lives like?

- What pressures do your parents face?

- If they both work, how do they divide the responsibilities at home such as cooking, cleaning, paying the bills, and so on?

- What is your dad's job title? (Answer these same questions for your mom if she has a job outside the home.)

- What does your dad actually do during the day?

- What is the hardest part of his job?

- What causes the most stress?

- What does he like about his job?

- Is this the job he really wants?

- If your mom stays at home, what is the hardest part of staying home for her?

- What household jobs and responsibilities does she do each day?

- Which does she enjoy most? Least?

- What types of volunteer or church activities does she

do during the week?

- What does your mom enjoy most about being at home?

If you can't answer these questions, talk with your parents. Find out if you can go to work with them for a day to see what they do.

Knowing about your parents' pasts and their present day-to-day lives helps you know more about them as people. You can learn what they like and don't like, the problems they've faced and overcome, and the factors that most influenced who they are today. God can give you the wisdom to understand your parents and the strength to be able to do your part to build a strong relationship with your parents. After all, parents were God's idea.

HERE'S WHAT YOU SAID

What factors make your parents the type of people that they are? Here's what some of you said:

"How they were raised and their belief in Jesus."

Micah Cleary, 11

"Their parents. The way they grew up."

Johnny Butler, 13

"Life experiences. That's how they became who they are. How their parents brought them up."

Esther Butler, 15

"How their parents raised them and having brothers and sisters and learning to get along with them. My parents know how to get along with others because they learned how to get along with brothers and sisters. Also being brought up in church makes a difference on the kind of people my parents are. They were brought up in church and now they are taking me to church."

Jewell Hembree, 12

"How their mom and dad raised them. How they got along with their brothers or sisters and how they learned to get along."

Raul Stephenson, 12

"The way their parents raised them, like what they were allowed to do and what rules they had at home."

Ashley Cassel, 15

FOLLOWING THROUGH

How much do you know about your parents? Finish the following sentences.

The thing that was hardest for my dad/mom growing up was:

_____

_____

_____

The thing my dad/mom liked most about his/her family growing up was:

_____

_____

_____

One thing my grandparents did that my dad/mom does the same is:

_____

_____

_____

_____

One thing my dad/mom said he/she would never do that his/her parents did was:

_____

_____

_____

My dad's/mom's number one goal for our family is:

_____

_____

_____

My parents have these goals and priorities for our family:

_____

_____

_____

Does your family have a mission statement? If not, perhaps you can write one together. All you need to do is write a sentence or two about what is most important to you and what you want to accomplish in your family life. If you can't write one with your parents, perhaps you can write your own statement about what you want from family life. Take time to do it now.

_____

_____

VERSES FOR THOUGHT

For the LORD gives wisdom, and from His mouth come knowledge and understanding.

Proverbs 2:6

Be completely humble and gentle; be patient, bearing with one another in love. Make every effort to keep the unity of the Spirit through the bond of peace.

Ephesians 4:2–3

Chapter 7

Improving Your Relationship with Your Parents

*D*o you get along with your parents? Do you feel they are your friends rather than enemies? Whether your relationship with your parents is poor or going pretty well, it can always be better. In this chapter we'll look at some ways you can improve your relationship with them.

Tim ran out the door letting it slam behind him. "I hate him," he muttered to himself.

"Tim, get back here right now!" his dad shouted angrily after him.

Tim spun around. "You never listen to me. You believe everything everyone else says about me, but you never believe me!"

"The note from your teacher says you disrupted class and haven't turned in your homework for a week," his dad replied.

"Did she mention that everyone was out of control, not just me? Did she tell you that I asked her for help with my homework but she didn't have time? No, she didn't! She tells you what she wants to and you believe her because she's the teacher," Tim said hotly.

"Well, maybe," his dad admitted. He took a deep breath before continuing. "The funny thing is, my dad did the same thing to me and I vowed I'd never do that to my kids. Maybe we'd better sit down and talk about this whole thing."

Tim hesitated, then walked back into the house and slumped down on the sofa. He tried to look nonchalant, but inside he felt a deep sense of relief that his dad was finally going to listen.

YOUR TURN

Tim's problem is common. Kids and parents often argue about school, siblings, and rules. Sometimes they forget to stop and work out the problems. Do you find yourself at odds with your parents? In this chapter you'll find some ways you can improve your relationship with them.

Keys to Improving Your Relationship with Your Parents

There are many ways you can improve your relationship with your parents. The keys below are general ideas. Use them as a starting point and tailor them to fit your family.

Act, don't react. In other words, think before you act. If your dad says you can't go to the football game with your friends and you immediately throw your backpack on the floor, stomp away, and slam a door—that's reacting. If you start screaming, "That's not fair, you never let me do anything"—that's reacting. Instead, stop and cool down. Think things through before you do anything. Then you can act in a more mature manner.

James 1:19–20 advises us, "My dear brothers, take note of this: Everyone should be quick to listen, slow to speak and slow to become angry, for man's anger does not bring about the righteous life that God desires." This is also good advice for dealing with parents.

Talk. Communication is a really important part of any relationship. If you don't talk to your parents, they won't know what's going on in your life. Sometimes it's easier to talk to a friend or sibling—they are closer to your age and may be facing the same problems you are. But try talking to your parents too.

Make sure the time is right when you talk to your parents about a disagreement. Wait until you have cooled off and can talk calmly. Avoid trying to have a discussion when people are angry, hungry, or tired. When people are angry, hungry, or tired, it is hard to concentrate and to think clearly. It's hard to keep tempers under control. Instead, wait until everyone is in a good mood to bring up a sticky subject. Chapter 8 has more suggestions for communication with your parents.

Listen. Don't just hear the words that come out of your parents' mouths, listen to the ideas and feelings behind the words. Look at your parents' body language. Do they look irritated, happy, or concerned? How they say things and how they look are sometimes just as important as the words they say.

Listen to your parents without interrupting or arguing. Hear them out. You want them to do the same thing for you when it's your turn to state your opinion or your side of a situation.

Compromise. Be willing to give in on the things that aren't really important. If your parents say you can't go to a party that you really didn't want to go to that badly anyway, give in and tell them you accept their decision. When something is really important to you, they will remember all the times you cooperated with their decisions in the past.

When you don't agree with your parents, try to work out a solution both of you like. Perhaps your parents won't let you go to a sleepover at a friend's house, but they would be willing to let you go for the evening and pick you up at 11:00. That's not what you want, but it's also not sitting at home missing the whole thing.

Pinpoint and resolve areas of conflict. Do you always fight with your parents about the same things? Television? Friends? Grades? Make a list of areas of conflict. What can you do to resolve the problems? Go through the first three keys again. Sit down and *talk* with your parents about these areas. *Listen* to their side of the story and be *willing to compromise.* If you can't talk with your parents, try talking to your pastor, youth leader, or other trusted adult.

Accept. Some things you just can't change. This is true for all of us, no matter what age. Even your parents face things they can't change such as work policies, paying taxes, laws, and rules of the road. The things we can't change we have to accept. Accepting them calmly shows maturity. When your parents see how mature you are becoming they may let you have more privileges or let you have your way more often.

HERE'S WHAT YOU SAID 📣

How can youth improve their relationship with their parents? Here's what some of you said:

> "You can improve your relationship with your parents by obeying them and honoring them. You can tell them when they have hurt your feelings. Don't take your anger out on people by getting into fights."
>
> Josiah Tharp, 9

> "Give them respect. They are in authority. Listen to what they say and don't argue because they've been through it before."
>
> James Rettew, 14

"Start by showing respect to your parents. Sometimes I get obnoxious to my parents. I get grounded and I deserve it."
David Rettew, 12

"Don't argue when your parents ask you to do chores such as mowing the lawn, doing dishes, weed whacking, and cleaning your room. If I argue my mom gives me an extra job to do too."
Raul Stephenson, 12

"Follow the rules so your parents will respect you."
Johnny Butler, 13

"Try to talk to them about what you think is cool. Talk to them about your life so that they will understand you better and you can get to understand them better."
Jewell Hembree, 12

"Talk to them."
Micah Cleary, 11

"Start by talking to them about your day and then work into talking about them about more important things."
Esther Butler, 15

"By talking to them. By telling them how you feel about things and listening to what they say."
Ashley Cassel, 15

FOLLOWING THROUGH

Are there times when you have difficulty getting along with your parents? What causes the most conflict?

_____

_____

If you could sit down and talk about this conflict with your parents, what would you say to them?

_____

_____

_____

What do you think they would say to you?

_____

_____

_____

What possible compromises could you make? What are *you* willing to do to solve the problem?

_____

_____

_____

According to the "Verses for Thought," what is the child's responsibility?

_____

_____

_____

What is God's promise?

_____

_____

_____

What is the father's responsibility? What does it mean?

_____

_____

Take time this week to talk over any existing conflicts with your parents. If you don't feel you can talk to them, talk with a pastor, youth leader, or other trusted adult.

VERSES FOR THOUGHT

Children obey your parents in the Lord, for this is right. "Honor your father and mother"—which is the first commandment with a promise—"that it may go well with you and that you may enjoy long life on the earth." Fathers, do not exasperate your children; instead, bring them up in the training and instruction of the Lord.

Ephesians 6:1–4

Above all, love each other deeply, because love covers over a multitude of sins.

1 Peter 4:8

Chapter 8

Improving Your Communication with Your Parents

Is it easier for you to talk to your friends than to your parents? Do you find it difficult to discuss daily events with your parents? Communicating with parents is important, but sometimes it takes a lot of work. In this chapter you'll find some ideas for improving your communication with your parents.

Liana flopped down on her bed. What a miserable day at school! Nothing had gone right. First, someone had started a rumor that she liked Brian the Brain. Everyone was laughing at her and singing out "Brian plus Liana" as she passed them. Then she got a D on her math test. She knew the D would get her a long lecture about living up to her potential and would probably mean she was grounded. On top of all that, her best friend, Allyson, was home sick so Liana couldn't talk to her about it.

Liana's mom knocked and entered the room. "Is anything wrong?" she asked.

"No," Liana answered.

"You seem upset. Are you sure there's nothing you want to talk about?" her mom asked again.

"I'm sure," Liana said.

After her mom left the room, Liana picked up her phone and dialed Allyson's number. "Boy, do I need to talk to you," Liana said. "This was a really awful day."

Your Turn

It's normal for teens to talk to their friends more than their family members, but staying in touch with your parents is important. Most likely, they really want to know what's going on in your life. If it's been a long time since you've talked to them or if you find it difficult to communicate with them, perhaps some of the suggestions below will help you get the lines open again.

Why It's Hard

There are many reasons why it's harder to talk to your parents now than it was when you were younger. Here are some possible reasons given by other teens:

- You are growing up. You don't always need to ask for help like you used to.

- Your life doesn't revolve around the family like it used to. You have your own activities and interests now.

- It's easier to talk to friends since you spend all day with them at school.

- It's easier to talk to friends because they don't criticize or nag at you.

- It's easier to talk to friends because they are involved in the same situations as you.

- You don't want to tell your parents everything. You want some privacy and freedom.

- Some of the really important things—such as God, sex, drugs, and relationships—are hard to talk about.

- You feel your parents wouldn't understand.

- You are afraid of getting in trouble if you tell them certain things.

- You don't know how to get started talking with your parents.
- Your parents seem too busy to talk.
- You feel too busy to talk.

Keep Talking

Even if you agree with some of the reasons above, it's still important to keep a line of communication open between you and your parents. Here are some ideas to help you do that.

Realize that you will disagree. Conflicts are part of growing up. You want to make your own decisions, but your parents want to offer guidance. This might lead to conflicts about places you are allowed to go alone, friends you can hang out with, how late you are allowed to stay out, what decisions you can make by yourself, how much time you can spend with friends and how much time you need to spend at home, and how much money you receive and what you can do with it. Sit down and talk when these situations occur.

Talk to your parents in a mature way. The best way to get them to listen is to show maturity. Whining, begging, and arguing aren't going to accomplish much. Be willing to listen and compromise.

Be calm. Choose a time when both you and your parents are calm and rested. Tell your parents how you feel about the conflict. Tell them why you feel that way and what solutions you can think of. Then listen while they tell you their ideas.

If you are upset or angry, take time to calm down before approaching your parents. Wait until you feel in control. Practice what you are going to say. You might even want to tape yourself so you can hear how you sound to your parents!

Remember the verses from James 1:19–20, "My dear brothers, take note of this: Everyone should be quick to listen, slow to speak and slow to become angry, for man's anger does not bring about the righteous life that God desires." Keep your temper in check and wait until you cool down to speak.

Talk about the important things. Even if you don't keep your parents up to date on the daily things such as which boy likes which girl, which girls are mad at each other, or who got invited to events and who didn't, talk to them about the important things. Talk to your parents about sex, drugs, peer pressure, and any abusive situations. Also talk to them about your goals, plans for the future, spiritual growth, and school problems. Let them know about the questions and problems you have. You may find they have some helpful advice.

Stay current. So many things happen between you and your friends and teachers each day it's hard to let your parents know everything. But as often as possible, let them know who your friends are and what activities are special to you.

Talk every day. Try to share one thing with your parents every day. If you are fortunate enough to eat supper together, you can make this a family activity. Choose one question for everyone to answer such as, "What was the best thing that happened today?" "What was the worst thing that happened today?" "If you could change one thing about today, what would it be?" Is it hard to just start talking with your parents? Try starting with some easy, fun subjects. Write out some questions on slips of paper and have each family member choose one to answer or all answer the same one. Write out questions such as, "If you could visit any place in the world, where would you go?" "If you inherited a million dollars, what would you do with it?" Don't think this would work? Give it a try before you discard the idea. Tailor it to fit your family.

Keep the lines open with God. Jesus talked with His Father regularly while He lived on earth. He prayed for Himself (see John 17:1–5), for others (see John 17:6–26) and for strength and confirmation in doing God's will (see Luke 22:41–44). We can pray for the same reasons.

Maybe you find it hard to sit still for a long period of time to pray. You're not alone! Realistically, it's hard for most of us to pray for a long time and listen for God to speak to us. Sometimes it's easier to pray off and on throughout the day. When you see a friend at school, say a quick prayer for him. When a friend shares a problem with you, say a silent prayer for her—or offer to pray aloud with her. When you're angry about something, ask God to help you control that anger. When you're in touch with God, things go better. After all, God cares about you more than anyone else does. He loves you so much He planned for your salvation before you were even born, and sacrificed His only Son for your forgiveness. Because He loves you so much, you can trust that He will hear your prayer, and guide you through difficult relationships.

Don't Give Up

Do you think some of these ideas would never work? Can't picture your family sitting around talking about what you'd each do with a million dollars? If you aren't used to talking together, it may be awkward at first. Maybe you could try starting a discussion in the car on the way to church each Sunday. Choose a topic that would create interest, such as things to do during school vacations or what one present everyone would like most for Christmas.

Don't give up! Through Christ, you can do anything. Ask Him to give you the courage to take the first steps towards communicating with your parents or as a family. He can help you keep the lines of communication open.

HERE'S WHAT YOU SAID

Do you talk to your parents about things that happen? Why or why not? Here's what some of you said:

"Yes. It makes it so that you're not hiding things you have done. If you hide things you've done, it hurts you. Talking to my parents can help me find truth. It can also help me do the right things."   Josiah Tharp, 9

"I always want to talk to my parents but if they aren't there I can talk to my brother-in-law because he gives me good advice."   Matthew Rettew, 11

"I talk to my dad most. We talk about the Bible and about what's happening in my life. If my dad's not around I talk to my mom about what's on my mind." David Rettew, 12

"I talk to them about what happens but I don't give them all the details. Some things I keep to myself. I have a pretty close relationship with my mom but some things I just want to keep to myself. Sometimes I think she wouldn't understand so I tell my friends instead."

Esther Butler, 15

"I talk to my parents because I don't have anyone else to talk to. I talk to them about everything."

Johnny Butler, 13

"I talk to my parents sometimes but I talk to my friends a lot because they are the same age and I can talk to them better." Jewell Hembree, 12

"I don't talk to them. My mom is very busy with my little sister. Also, we always get into a fight when we talk so I talk to my friend Nikki. She listens to me and understands me." Ashley Cassel, 15

FOLLOWING THROUGH

How are you at talking with your parents? Use this scale to rate yourself on the following sentences:

1–Never	4–Most of the time
2–Rarely	5–Always
3–Sometimes	

___ I can talk to my parents even when we disagree on things.

___ I talk to my parents about the things that are most important to me.

___ I keep my parents up to date on what's happening in my life.

___ I talk to my parents in a mature way.

___ I take time to talk to God about my life.

___ Total

Your Score

20–25 You are doing a good job at communicating with your parents. Keep it up!

15–20 You are making an effort but there is room for improvement. Work on weak areas.

Below 15 You are having difficulty in communicating with your parents. Give serious thought to the things talked about in the chapter. Seek help if needed.

Make a plan to tell your parents one thing that happens at school each day this week. What types of things will you tell them? How? When?

_____

_____

_____

Are there some important things that you need to share with your parents? What? How and when will you talk to them?

_____

_____

_____

What things can you do to improve communication with your parents? With your whole family?

_____

_____

_____

VERSES FOR THOUGHT

Let your conversation be always full of grace, seasoned with salt, so that you may know how to answer everyone.

Colossians 4:6

And the God of all grace, who called you to His eternal glory in Christ, after you have suffered a little while, will Himself restore you and make you strong, firm and steadfast.

1 Peter 5:10

siblings

Chapter 9

All Kinds of Siblings

Siblings come in all shapes, sizes, ages, and personality types. They can be siblings by birth, remarriage of parents, adoption, or foster care. Some siblings are easy to get along with, others aren't. You may have a lot or nothing in common with your siblings. In this chapter we'll look at sibling relationships.

Dominic dribbled the soccer ball, aimed, and kicked. Goal! Dominic smiled half-heartedly. Soccer was okay, but it wasn't his real passion—football was. But Carlos was the star of the football team and Dominic was tired of following in his steps, tired of hearing how great Carlos was. So Dominic chose to play the one sport Carlos wasn't any good at.

The game ended with a score of 3–2. Dominic had made two out of the three goals for his team and assisted the other goal.

"Way to go," his friend Derek said, slapping him on the back in congratulations.

"Yeah, thanks," Dominic said.

"You don't sound very excited about the game," Derek said.

"It was okay," Dominic replied.

Derek laughed. "Man, it was more than okay. You had some great footwork."

Dominic shrugged. He knew he should feel proud, but all he felt was annoyed—annoyed that he was playing a sport he didn't really want to play, annoyed at

Carlos for being the older brother, annoyed at Carlos for being so good at everything. The thing was, it wasn't even Carlos who pointed out how good he was at everything, it was their mother. To her, Carlos was perfect.

Dominic knew he would never mention the goals he had scored to his family. They had never even been to one of his games. He sighed and started toward home.

YOUR TURN

What kind of siblings do you have? Older? Younger? Stepsiblings? Half siblings? Is your relationship the same with all of your siblings? Many things can influence your relationship with your siblings. What most influences your relationship with each of your siblings?

Siblings—Alike and Different

Approximately 80 percent of all Americans have siblings. Sibling relationships continue for the rest of your life. Sometimes adult siblings choose not to stay in touch with one another. Perhaps a quarrel has separated them or they may find they have little in common. But often sibling relationships outlast friendships and even marriages. Some people think brothers and sisters play a very small role in our lives. Others argue sibling relationships have a big impact on how we feel about ourselves, how we feel about others, and what kind of person we are as an adult.

Rivalry and competition between siblings is normal—even healthy at times. But when rivalry goes too far it can turn into serious hostility. Physical or verbal abuse suffered at the hands of a sibling can leave scars well into adulthood.

Sibling relationships allow brothers and sisters to learn

problem-solving skills and how to resolve conflicts. Siblings become built-in playmates during younger years and companions during later years. Sometimes siblings become close friends, other times when one sibling is much older he becomes more of a role model than friend and companion. An older sibling may also take on some parental responsibilities for much younger siblings.

Sometimes people expect brothers and sisters who are raised together with the same rules, values, social class, and parents to be very much alike. This isn't always true. The experiences individual children have, how they perceive people and situations, and their own personality make them unique from their siblings. Even birth order can play a part in making each sibling individual. We'll talk more about that in the next chapter.

Because siblings are so different, they may not all relate to one another in the same way. You may find it easier to get along with one sibling than with another. Many factors determine how well you get along with each individual sibling.

Factors That Influence Sibling Relationships

Here are some factors that affect how well you get along with your siblings:

Age How close in age you are to your brothers and sisters is one factor that influences your relationships. The closer you are in age, the more you may have in common. You attend the same school, know the same kids, share the same school activities and teachers. But being close in age can also mean competitiveness. Perhaps your sister who is a year older than you is very popular and you aren't. Or maybe your younger brother is a genius and you aren't. Siblings close in age often get compared to each other, which may affect their relationship.

Interests If you share the same hobbies as your siblings, you are likely to have a better relationship with them. You enjoy shooting baskets, collecting stamps, riding bikes, or going to karate class together. This gives you things to talk about and work on together. If you don't have much in common with your siblings, you may have more of a problem talking with them or hanging out with them.

Personality types Some people naturally get along well together while others get on each other's nerves. Personality types have much to do with this. Perhaps you don't like to get up early, but your little sister does. While you're spooning cereal into your mouth, still fast asleep, she is talking 100 words a minute. Maybe you like things neat and organized but are sharing your room with a brother more interested in always doing things with his friends. He doesn't want to waste time organizing. These types of personality differences can lead to conflict.

Background Whether you are biological, step, adopted, or foster siblings makes a difference. Sometimes it takes a while to get used to a new brother or sister. He or she may have different ways of doing things or even different values. Or perhaps it is easier to get along with someone who is new to you. You find yourself becoming friends as well as siblings.

Gender Maybe you get along better with siblings who are the same sex as you, or maybe you get along better with the ones who are the opposite sex. Same-sex siblings can relate better to the things you are going through, but often you have more rivalry with them.

Parents How your parents taught you to get along when you were younger also affects how well you get along now. If they helped you care about one anothers' feelings and work out problems together, you may relate better to one another now. How your parents treat you and your siblings also makes a difference. For instance, you may notice they let your little sister do things you aren't allowed to. This affects how you feel about her, and how you may treat her.

Special needs Sometimes having siblings with special needs adds stress to sibling relationships. Special-needs siblings require extra care and possibly many trips to doctors or specialists. They may need special schooling. This can cause additional expenses for a family, and you may have to go without something you wanted, which builds up resentment. At the same time, you may have the chance to develop special relationships with them that you wouldn't with other siblings.

HERE'S WHAT YOU SAID

Do you get along better with one of your siblings than the other(s)? Why or why not? Here's what some of you said:

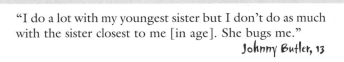

"I get along with my youngest brother the best because he is nicer and he is easier to get along with. One of my brothers is just learning to speak English so we have to help him understand things. That is sometimes frustrating."
Tyler Cassel, 8

"I do a lot with my youngest sister but I don't do as much with the sister closest to me [in age]. She bugs me."
Johnny Butler, 13

"I don't have any brothers or sisters but I wish I did.

Sometimes being an only child gets lonely and I have to wait until school to have other kids to talk to."

Jewell Hembree, 12

"I get along with all of them at different times but some of the personalities get on my nerves. I never get jealous of any of them. I get along with my oldest brother pretty well but we're so much alike that we fight a lot."

Esther Butler, 15

"I get along with all of them. Some of the little guys can't do much so I do more with the ones that can play football and soccer. But I do other things with the little ones."

Matthew Rettew, 11

"I get along with all 20 of them. I play outside with some of them and the ones that can't play watch and we do different things with them."

David Rettew, 12

"I get along with all of them the same. We understand each other. I do different things with some of them because some of them have special needs and we have to be careful of them. I try to spend time with all of them every day but I have a lot of brothers and sisters and some-times it is hard to spend time with all of them. I help some of them with the things they need help with and I play soccer with some of them." **James Rettew, 14**

Following Through

List each of your siblings along the edge of this chart. Then fill in the squares.

Names of siblings	Age	Things in common	Things we fight about

With which of your siblings do you get along best? Why?

_____

_____

_____

Are there ways you can find more in common with your siblings?

_____

_____

_____

Read the 1 Corinthians verse in "Verses for Thought." How does this apply to you and your siblings, whether you are similar or not?

_____

_____

_____

How can you be a help and encouragement to each of your siblings?

_____

_____

VERSES FOR THOUGHT

Love must be sincere. Hate what is evil: cling to what is good. Be devoted to one another in brotherly love. Honor one another above yourselves.

Romans 12:9–10

There are different kinds of gifts, but the same Spirit. There are different kinds of service, but the same Lord. There are different kinds of working, but the same God works all of them in all men.

1 Corinthians 12:4–6

Chapter 10

What Difference Does Birth Order Make?

*D*oes it make a difference whether you are an oldest, middle, or youngest child? Sometimes. While there is no perfect formula, some characteristics are shared by oldest, middle, and youngest children. There are also other factors that make siblings different from one another.

> *Eric woke with a start. "Hungry, Eric, hungry," his sister was saying, tugging on his pillow to wake him up. "Want breakfast now."*
>
> *"Go away, Brittany. I'm tired. Let me sleep."*
>
> *"Hungry Eric. Want breakfast!" she demanded.*
>
> *Eric rolled over and looked at the clock—7:10 a.m.. What a way to start summer vacation, fixing breakfast for his little sister before 8:00. Maybe if he was lucky he could get her to watch cartoons and he could sleep on the couch.*
>
> *Eric poured Cheerios for Brittany and gave her a glass of juice. "Don't spill anything, okay? I don't want to clean up anything this early." Eric got his own bowl of cereal and sat down to eat. He liked the extra spending money his mom was giving him to watch Brittany, but he wasn't sure he was going to like fixing meals, cleaning her up, and entertaining her all day.*
>
> *"I guess it's part of being the oldest," Eric told himself, turning on Brittany's favorite television show. "I get to watch a purple dinosaur sing and dance all summer!"*

Your Turn

Maybe you are the firstborn child. Perhaps you're the middle of many children. You might be the youngest, or one of the youngest. Maybe you are an only child. Does this make a difference? Not everyone agrees that birth order makes a difference in the type of person you become. Read this chapter and decide for yourself.

General Characteristics

Why is it that siblings with similar genetic makeup, who share the same family environment, values, rules, and experiences can be so different?

Some people think birth order doesn't really make a difference, that you will have whatever characteristics you have no matter whether you are the first, middle, or last child. They believe your own personality, how you interact with the world, and your individual experiences are what determine the kind of person you are. But other people who have studied the characteristics of children in relationship to birth order say it does make a difference. They have seen the same characteristics among children sharing the same position in the family.

The very first person to do research about birth order and share his beliefs was Dr. Alfred Adler, an Austrian psychiatrist born in 1870. He came from a family of five children. Dr. Adler was the second child and also the second boy. He felt inferior to his bigger, stronger, older brother. He believed that whether a person was a firstborn, secondborn, thirdborn, or later child was important to his development.

A Look at Birth Order

The information below is a generalization of the different birth order positions. If you want to learn more about birth order there are several books about it available in libraries and bookstores.

Oldest child As the firstborn child, you got all your parents' attention at least for a short amount of time, sometimes for a long period of time. You usually have a good relationship with your parents. You also have seniority among your siblings. You learn how to do things first and are the first to face new experiences such as going to school, driving, and dating. You may have more privileges and more responsibilities than your younger siblings.

Since you were the first child, your parents may not have known what to expect. They probably have had unrealistically high expectations for you. They may seem to expect you to be perfect the first time you try something, and expect you to keep achieving perfection in grades and sports. Your parents may also be more protective of you than they are of your siblings.

Because of the close interaction you've had with your parents, you're often responsible, goal-oriented, and highly motivated. You tend to be confident and successful, and are a good leader.

Teresa Cleary, a mother of three, says, "I have seen a birth order difference in terms of personalities of my children. Micah, 11, is the conscientious, take-charge firstborn. I see Micah taking charge when we are away from home. He makes sure Emily, 5, doesn't walk too far away by taking her hand or keeping an eye on her. He does the same with Steven, 8, but in a much more 'bossy' way. Emily loves the attention from Micah but Steven reacts with 'You're not the boss.' Sometimes I find myself telling him, 'You're not the mom' when he takes charge or gets too bossy."

Not all firstborn children follow the general rule. Kristie Butler has six children. She doesn't think her oldest child, a boy, fits the stereotype, but her second child, a girl, does. "I think birth order follows the tradition that firstborns take more initiative, but my firstborn doesn't have that characteristic as much as our second child. Esther is like a second firstborn. She has more of the firstborn characteristics than our true firstborn does. She is also a very mothering person."

Here are some more characteristics you might have as a firstborn child:

- Capable
- Strong willed
- Responsible
- Secure
- Confident
- Competitive
- Dominant

Middle child Middle children are more difficult to stereotype since a lot will depend on your older sibling(s) and the way your parents raised you. For instance, you may not have gotten as much attention for walking and talking as an older sibling did. Some of the novelty of having a child has worn off for your parents, which means less attention for you. But it also means your parents are becoming more relaxed and realistic, which makes it easier to grow up at your own pace.

Sometimes as a middle child you try to be completely

opposite from the firstborn child to have your own place in your family. You create your own ways to stand out in your family to avoid being overlooked. But if you're a different gender than your older sibling, you may not feel the need to find a way to get more attention.

Teresa Cleary said, "Steven is the do-anything-for-attention middle child who likes to test the limits. If I say, 'Be home at 8:00,' I can count on going out to find him at 8:05. It seems like everything he does is for attention. But he is very affectionate and likes to sit with me and snuggle. I think he craves the attention the other two get for being the oldest and the baby of the family. I see a need for more 'mom time' with him than the other two. He does express that to me rather than just getting resentful about it all."

Kristie Butler feels two of her six children have middle-child characteristics. "Johnny has annoying attention-getting habits," Kristie says. "He stands too close to you, cracks his knuckles, and makes constant noises. If he's in the room you know it." His attention getting also has a positive side. "He's very willing to help. He's the first one to help carry in the groceries or do an extra job. He never grumbles about it.

"Mary is the opposite in her attention getting," Kristie continues. "She is a 'space-cadet,' but it's an attention-getting thing. We will all be in the car waiting for her or in the living room waiting for her. Her favorite lines are 'I forgot' or 'I didn't know.' It annoys the others. But she's also the very best friend someone could have. She is even friends with those who don't have any other friends."

Here are some more characteristics you might have as a middle child:

- Spontaneous
- Easygoing

- Flexible
- Relaxed
- Tactful
- Patient

Youngest child As the youngest child in the family, you have a reputation for being spoiled or getting extra attention. Is this really true? Maybe. By the time you were born, the novelty of first steps and first words definitely has worn off. Your older siblings may have photo albums crammed full of pictures taken of each milestone, while there are only a few photographs of you at holiday events.

Usually this is because your parents were much more relaxed by the time they had you. They realize that children aren't as breakable as they thought, so you may have more freedom and less parental scrutiny. In later years, you'll follow your siblings' footsteps in dating and learning to drive. Your parents are over their nervousness about these events, which will make it easier for you.

Although you may receive less parental attention, you have the benefit of older siblings to do things for you. Sometimes your siblings will be the ones to teach you how to tie your shoes or will get you breakfast in the morning. But at the same time, you will always live in the shadows of your siblings, and have to compete with them to establish your own identity. Because of this, you sometimes turn to clowning around or being charming to gain attention.

Teresa Cleary says, "Emily is the I'm-the-baby-and-I-get-away-with-more-than-my-brothers-ever-dreamed-of thirdborn. She is a born manipulator and knows she can get away with it because we have relaxed our standards and are too tired to care a lot of the time. As the youngest, she also reaps the benefits of having everyone in the house available to take care of her. If Mom or Dad are busy there are still two big brothers to ask to do something for her."

Of her two youngest of six children, Kristie Butler finds only one of them has the characteristics of the youngest child. "Michaela is definitely the baby of the family. She lets everybody do anything for her. She's so cute she gets away with anything. The older kids never see what she does wrong. Her best friend is her big brother Albert. She knows all the teens he hangs around with because Albert takes her with him places. Michaela has many people spoiling her."

Here are some more characteristics you might have as a youngest child:

- Accepting
- Attention seeking
- Popular with peers
- Secure
- Easygoing

Special cases The rules for birth order don't always work. If you are the only child, you don't really have a birth order. You will often take on the characteristics of a firstborn child.

If you're a twin, triplet, or other multiple, you don't really fit the pattern either. A problem for you may be that you tend to get treated just like your sibling(s), even though you are different.

If you want to learn more about how you fit the birth order stereotype you might want to read *The New Birth Order Book: Why You Are the Way You Are,* by Dr. Kevin Lehman (Revell, 1998).

How Does Birth Order Affect Sibling Relationships?

If birth order really affects families, then it will affect sibling relationships.

If you're the firstborn child, being bigger and older, you may be bossy with younger siblings. Since you may get blamed when your younger siblings fight or misbehave, you may find ways to make sure younger siblings behave correctly. You may also have the responsibility to help care for younger siblings.

As the secondborn, you're used to not getting things your own way so you're often more relaxed in your relationships with siblings. If you're a competitive person, you may spend a lot of time trying to compete with the older, larger, firstborn child. This can lead to frequent fighting.

As the youngest, or younger child, you are used to being pushed around by older siblings. You are also used to having older siblings take care of you. You may have found it is easiest to learn to get along with older siblings than fight them.

Does Birth Order Really Matter?

In many cases people do display the characteristics talked about above, but this isn't always true. We all have our own personalities, and not all parents treat their children the way birth order theories assume they do. Perhaps you're the firstborn and your parents don't have unrealistic expectations for you—they encourage you to be yourself and grow up at your own rate. Or maybe your parents treat you and your siblings exactly the same. Many different factors will affect who you are and how you act.

One thing is for sure. When God, our Heavenly Father, looks at you, He sees you, through Christ, as His special and redeemed child. He created you with all the characteristics, talents, and abilities that make you unique from your siblings. Take time to thank God for making you who you are, and ask His forgiveness for all the times you haven't appreciated who He made you to be. He will forgive you, and help you to realize just how special you are, whether you are a first-, middle-, or lastborn child.

HERE'S WHAT YOU SAID

Does it make a difference if you are the oldest, middle, or youngest child? What are you and how does that affect you? Here's what some of you said:

"It doesn't make a difference. I'm the oldest but I don't have to do more than the others. We all have our own jobs to do and the same rules. Sometimes my sister and I do get to do more than the little boys though, like stay up later or go play at a friend's house." **Tyler Cassel, 8**

"Usually the oldest is more responsible, but I'm really more responsible than my brother. I can cook and take care of myself better than him. My mom trusts me to take care of things for her like returning videos." **Raul Stephenson, 12**

"I'm the second oldest but I'm the oldest girl. My parents haven't been through some things before that they go through with me so it'll be easier for my younger sisters. I do more of the work and have more responsibility than the little girls." **Esther Butler, 15**

"I don't mind being in the middle. My parents have gone through a lot with my older brother so I get away with more than he did." **Johnny Butler, 13**

"I'm the oldest. My sister is only 2 so I have all the responsibility."
Ashley Cassel, 15

"Being firstborn I usually get in trouble when things happen and I am expected to do more chores and stuff. I also get more privileges like getting to ride my bike farther, staying up later, and watching more movies than my brother and sister."
Micah Cleary, 11

Following Through

How many children are in your family?___
Which number child are you?___
Are you the only child of your sex in the family?___
How many years are there between each of your siblings and yourself?

_____

_____

Do you think that you and your siblings fit the descriptions of oldest, middle, and youngest children given in this chapter? Which characteristics best describe you and your siblings?

Oldest child

_____

_____

_____

Middle child or children

_____

_____

Youngest child or children

_____

_____

_____

Read 1 Corinthians 12:12–20. Paul is talking about all of God's people working together, but how do these verses apply to your particular family?

_____

_____

_____

Share this chapter with your parents and see if they agree with your insights.

VERSES FOR THOUGHT

For You created my inmost being; You knit me together in my mother's womb. I praise You because I am fearfully and wonderfully made; Your works are wonderful, I know that full well.

Psalm 139:13–14

But in fact God has arranged the parts in the body, every one of them, just as He wanted them to be. If they were all one part, where would the body be? As it is, there are many parts, but one body.

1 Corinthians 12:18–20

Chapter 11

Sibling Squabbles

Most siblings fight, some more than others. That's pretty normal. In this chapter we'll look at some reasons siblings fight, how to avoid fighting, and how to fight fair when a fight does break out.

> *"Your junk is on my side of the room again!" Mary Kate yelled at her sister Tanya. "Get it off my side!"*
>
> *"Well, you have more room than me," Tanya yelled back. "And besides, my stuff's not on your side, it's on my side."*
>
> *"That's not your side. And anyway, the closet is on my side so I always have you running around my side of the room."*
>
> *"Oh, grow up!" Tanya said. "You are such a baby!"*
>
> *"At least I'm not a slob!" Mary Kate yelled.*
>
> *"Well, if you're so worried about sides, watch this," Tanya said. She picked up a black marker off her desk, yanked off the lid, and started to draw a black line on the floor.*
>
> *"Tanya! What are you doing?"*
>
> *"I'm making sure we each know whose side is whose," Tanya replied.*
>
> *"Boy are you going to be in trouble when mom sees that," Mary Kate said.*
>
> *"Fine. But now you can stay on your own side of the room!"*

Your Turn

Are there definite things that cause bickering between you and your siblings? You may not be able to solve all the problems and eliminate fighting, but you can reduce the number of fights and learn to fight fairly when you do fight.

Why Fight?

Why do sibling fights take place? There are many understandable reasons.

Togetherness You are with siblings more than with anyone else. You have to listen to your sister bragging about her schoolwork or new boyfriend, and you have to share a bathroom with her. You have to listen to your brother talk about his great football play and step over his dirty football uniform to get into the bathroom. All this togetherness naturally leads to fighting.

Territorial rights Along with being together a lot, sometimes territorial rights are violated. Your little brother enters your room without permission and gets into all your stuff. Your older brother borrows your favorite CD without asking, or turns on his favorite television program when it is your night to choose the show. Your sister reads your diary and tells all her friends what it says, or borrows your favorite sweater and forgets to return it.

Attention Some fights take place simply for attention. It may seem that you have to compete for your parents' love and attention, and starting a fight seems like a good way to get attention, even if it's negative.

Competition A fight may take place if one sibling gets a privilege or possession the others don't. It may seem that one sibling is better liked or treated more fairly. Competition for friends, grades, and popularity at school can also lead to fighting.

Anger Your anger may not be because of a sibling, but may be because of a school problem such as a fight with a friend or a poor grade. Since siblings are right there in the house with you, they often get the worst of it. You may also feel it's safer to take it out on them.

Physical factors When you are tired, hungry, or fatigued from sports practice, you are more likely to fight. This is why many fights occur right before supper. You've spent all day in school sitting at a desk, working on difficult subject matter, you're hungry, and you feel out of sorts. It doesn't take much to start a fight over even the most trivial things.

Avoiding Fights

Looking at the reasons for fights can help you come up with ideas to avoid them. Here are some possible suggestions.

Separate. If you are together at school, home, church, and sports events, it may be time for some separate activities. Look for things you can do away from home and siblings. Branch out from shared activities. If your brother is going to be on the yearbook staff, sign up for drama instead. If your sister is a cheerleader, sign up for the dance team or join the basketball team. Avoid being in all the same activities.

Create your own space. Having your own room helps cut down on problems with siblings. If this isn't possible, you can still create a space of your own. Try to divide your room using furniture. Maybe you can build a wall using desks and bookcases, or perhaps you can design a partition of some sort or hang a curtain to create a private corner.

Talk to your parents about the possibilities. If this doesn't work, maybe you can claim another area of the house as your own.

Take turns! Create schedules for bathroom time, choosing television shows, and other things that cause conflict. When you are faced with choices such as who gets the last soda, flip a coin and accept the outcome.

Use your energy constructively. Look for other outlets for your energy when you feel a fight brewing. Jog a couple of miles, go for a bike ride, hit a tennis ball against the garage, or shoot baskets. Use your energy constructively instead of channeling it into a fight.

Refuel. Take time to relax and refuel after school or after tiring activities. Grab an apple, go to your room, and listen to your favorite CD before facing siblings. Take a break before tackling homework or household chores (with your parents' permission of course).

Rules for a Fair Fight

Fighting with siblings is a normal part of growing up. You can fight fair by fighting without hurting the other person. Here are some guidelines to follow.

Avoid name-calling. Calling each other names doesn't do any good—in fact, it does a lot of harm. Usually name-calling is meant to insult your sibling. Names like "brace face" or "idiot" make fun of something about your sibling, or label your sibling in an unfair way. Name-calling shows a lack of respect for the other person. Leave name-calling out of the fight.

Avoid cutdowns. Cutdowns are similar to name-calling in that they show a lack of respect and cause hurt feelings. Comments like, "You're so stupid you ..." and similar ones should be banned from fights. Fighting needs to lead to a solution, and slamming each other won't accomplish that.

Listen to each other's side of the argument. Tell your side of the problem and then listen while your brother or sister tells his or her side. Make sure each of you understands the other person's point of view. If you can't do this peacefully you may need a parent to referee to make sure both sides are heard and are told as truthfully as possible.

Avoid physical involvement. Kicking, hitting, and pushing don't lead to a peaceful resolution of the problem, especially if one person has a size advantage. If anger becomes a problem, get away from each other until you cool down. Jog, shoot baskets, or do something else to get rid of the extra energy created by your anger.

Attack the problem not the person. Keep in mind that solving the problem—not destroying the person—is the goal.

Resolve the problem by bedtime. Don't let anger, hard feelings, or hurt carry over into the next day. Ephesians 4:26 says, "In your anger do not sin. Do not let the sun go down while you are still angry." Carrying over anger and hurt feelings isn't healthy. It can make you sick physically and hurt you emotionally.

Forgive and forget. Once the fight is over, it's over. Don't bring it up again later. Forgive others just as Christ forgave us—completely and forever. Jesus died on the cross not only to forgive our sins, but also so that through Him, we will have the ability to forgive others. Ask Him for help if you find it hard to forgive your siblings. He will help you!

Seek peace. Even though fighting is normal among siblings, strive for peaceful times. Jesus said, "Peace I leave with you; My peace I give you" (John 14:27). Through the Holy Spirit, Jesus will give you His peace during the time you don't feel peaceful yourself. If you have Jesus' peace within yourself, it will be easier to keep peace with those around you.

Here's What You Said

What do you fight about? How do you end or resolve fights with siblings? Here's what some of you said:

"We fight about stuff like toys, who gets the front seat in the car, and who's right. Usually Steven runs and tells on me and my parents take care of it." **Micah Cleary, 11**

"I fight with my brother because he usually takes my stuff and annoys me and hogs the computer. We throw punches and call each other names until my mom stops us."
Raul Stephenson, age 12

"My parents step in and help us to solve the fights the right way. They start by asking us what happened. Then they have us talk about it. Then they have us tell each other we are sorry and that we forgive the other person."
Josiah Tharp, 9

"We fight about different stuff. Sometimes they just get on my nerves and I hit them. They go tell and I get into trouble." **Johnny Butler, 13**

"We fight, but only about little silly stuff. We pray about it and then go back and talk to the other person."
David Rettew, 12

"Most of the time we fight over silly stuff. We walk away

or go and talk to our parents. Sometimes we try to solve it by ourselves and that doesn't work as well."
Matthew Rettew, 11

"I fight with my older brother over CDs, TV, and opinions. We don't really resolve it, we just go on. We let it go. With the younger ones we fight about cleaning up and keeping out of my personal space. I yell at them or tell my parents."
Esther Butler, 15

FOLLOWING THROUGH

What do you fight about most often?

How could this be avoided?

Which of the rules for a fair fight could help you?

What advice do the "Verses for Thought" give about ending fights and forgivness?

If your fighting is more serious than just fights about which television show to watch or who gets the last piece of cake, talk to your parents, pastor, or school counselor. They can give you more ideas about how to get along.

Verses for Thought

A gentle answer turns away wrath, but a harsh word stirs up anger. The tongue that brings healing is a tree of life, but a deceitful tongue crushes the spirit.

Proverbs 15:1, 4

Be kind and compassionate to one another, forgiving each other, just as in Christ God forgave you.

Ephesians 4:32

Chapter 12

Improving Sibling Relationships

Most sibling relationships have some flaws. Sibling fights are normal, but it's also good to work on strengthening your relationships with your brothers and sisters. These relationships can last into your adult years and have a major influence on your life. In this chapter, we'll look at how to work together to improve sibling relationships.

Jordan felt a pang of jealousy as he watched Josh fasten the belt on his karate gi and pull the knot tight.

Josh noticed Jordan was watching him and gave his brother a sarcastic smile. "I think the belt looks good on me," he said with a laugh.

"Show-off," Jordan said.

"What do you mean?" Josh asked, pretending innocence.

"You think you're so tough ever since you got your brown belt and I missed it," Jordan said. "But you're no better than me."

"Well, if you didn't goof off so much you would have your brown belt too."

"I don't goof off," Jordan said. "You're just the teacher's pet. You're everyone's pet. They think since you're so quiet you're good, but I know the truth. You do as much bad stuff as I do, you just don't get caught."

"You're just stupid—that's why you get caught," Josh said.

Jordan looked at his brother and felt his anger rise.

He was always the one in trouble whenever anything happened, whether it was his fault or not. It had been that way at home and school for as long as he could remember. Sure, he goofed around at times and mouthed off to his parents and teachers more than he should, but Josh was no saint either.

Jordan turned and executed a side kick toward his brother. Josh blocked it and said, "No-no, little brother, karate is for defense only."

Jordan turned away, angrier than ever. Why did God have to make brothers anyway?

Your Turn

Are there times when you wonder why God made brothers or sisters? Most everyone feels that way at times. Some sibling relationships may be so bad that outside help is needed to solve the problems, but for the most part any sibling relationship can be improved by putting the following ideas into practice.

Tips for Improving Sibling Relationships

The following suggestions are just a few ideas to get you started. Think of more that may help you.

Respect others. Everyone should be treated as a person who has value to God and others. Even if you don't get along, show respect for your sibling's character, feelings, and belongings.

Be responsible. Be responsible for your own words and actions. No fair saying you hit your brother because he hit you first. That isn't being responsible for your own actions. The same goes for saying you called your brother a name because he called you one. Another part of being responsible is doing your fair share of the work. When one sibling ends up doing most of the work, fights break out. If it seems like you have more than your fair share of the work, talk to your mom or dad about it.

Relate. Try to understand your sibling's point of view and feelings. If you don't understand, ask him to explain his feelings. You don't have to agree with him, but you do need to accept his feelings are his own whether you agree with them or not. Everyone is different and has different emotions and even different reactions to the same problems.

Relinquish. Let go of bad feelings and grudges. Don't carry yesterday's baggage with you. If you hold on to past bad feelings, you will dwell on them and start looking for a way to get even. You may use them to excuse yourself from trying to improve the relationship.

Cheer. Get on the same team. Don't try to undermine a sibling. Give her support and encouragement and expect the same from her. A family should be a place where you can find unconditional love and acceptance. It should also be a place where everyone is on your side and wants the best for you. The Bible encourages us to "Rejoice with those who rejoice" (Romans 12:15). Do your part to make this happen in your home. Remember: Christ gives you the strength to do anything, especially when you don't have the heart or the energy. He is on your side, cheering for you, as you cheer or the members of your family.

HERE's WHAT YOU SAID

What would help siblings get along better? Here's what some of you said:

"A miracle. It's not going to happen."
Raul Stephenson, age 12

"Read what the Bible says about loving each other. We don't fight much. We are out singing together for Jesus and there isn't much time to get into trouble with each other."
David Rettew, 12

"Try to help each other and not tear each other down. Talk with each other and try to get along. I think brothers and sisters would get along better if they'd listen instead of fighting. Fighting gets you nowhere."
James Rettew, 14

"If they could agree on things by trying not to argue and listening to each other's side." Micah Cleary, 11

"Finding things to do together that everyone likes and doing things together as a family. We all do church activities together and go fun places together." Tyler Cassel, 8

"Listening to each other and not fighting over the little things. I think brothers and sisters should try to get along because you will always be related. When my little sister gets bigger I hope she will talk to me about her problems and I can help her." Ashley Cassel, 15

"Siblings would get along better if they read the Bible more. It would also help if the parents would teach them to respect others." Aaron Tharp, 11

FOLLOWING THROUGH

What causes the most conflicts between you and your siblings?

What possible solutions can you think of to resolve the conflicts?

_____

_____

What things do you enjoy doing with your siblings? What new things could you do together?

_____

_____

Below are the steps listed for improving your relationship with your siblings. Rate yourself on how well you do in each area. You may want to score separately for each sibling.

1–Never	4–Most of the time
2–Rarely	5–Always
3–Sometimes	

___I respect my siblings' feelings and belongings.
___I take responsibility for my actions.
___I take responsibility for work I am to do.
___I try to relate to my siblings.
___I root for my siblings.
___Total

Your Score

20–25 You are doing a good job getting along with your siblings. Keep it up!

15–20 You are making an effort but there is room for improvement. Work on weak areas.

Below 15 You are having difficulty in getting along with siblings. Talk to your parents, youth pastor, or counselor for ideas on improving these relationships.

Verses for Thought

"The LORD Himself goes before you and will be with you; He will never leave you nor forsake you. Do not be afraid; do not be discouraged."

Deuteronomy 31:8

Do not repay anyone evil for evil. Be careful to do what is right in the eyes of everybody. If it is possible, as far as it depends on you, live at peace with everyone.

Romans 12:17–18

Discussion Questions

Chapter 1

1. How would you define the word *family*?
2. Who makes up your family?
3. Is your family the same or different from most of your friends' families?
4. Which of the youth that you read about in this chapter is most like yourself?

Chapter 2

1. Why did God create the family unit?
2. How do you think families have changed?
3. How is your family different from those in which your parents were raised?
4. Has God's plan for families changed?

Chapter 3

1. How would it feel to live in a single-parent, adoptive, or mixed race family?
2. How would it feel to live with a relative other than your parents or in a foster family?
3. What challenges do these families face?
4. What advantages do they have?

Chapter 4

1. What do you think is the most important value a family can have?
2. How does this value create happiness?
3. How can you help your family share this value?
4. Can families that don't have this value be truly happy?

Chapter 5

1. Do you agree or disagree that the parental roles are disciplinarian, provider, example, nurturer, guidance couselor, and faith nurturer?
2. Which role is most important for your parents to fulfill?
3. How do they do this, or how should they do this?
4. What other roles can they play?

Chapter 6

1. What was happening in the world when your parents grew up?
2. What kind of family did your parents come from?
3. Why does this make a difference?
4. What other things make your parents who they are today?

Chapter 7

1. Why are both talking and listening important?
2. What other things besides your parents' words give you clues about how they really feel?
3. What are some areas of conflict between youth and parents?
4. Why is compromise important?

Chapter 8

1. Who do you talk to the most—friends or parents? Why?
2. Why is it sometimes easier to talk to friends?
3. When is it better to talk to parents rather than friends?
4. What would make it easier for you to talk to your parents?

Chapter 9

1. Do you think siblings play an important role in the lives of their brothers and sisters?

2. Are siblings who are raised with the same values, rules, and parents, who are alike? If no, explain.
3. Do you get along better with one of your siblings than another? Why or why not?
4. How can you be a positive influence on your siblings?

Chapter 10

1. Do you think birth order makes a difference in a family? Why or why not?
2. What other factors make you who you are?
3. Do you see the birth order characteristics in your own life—if you are a firstborn do you see the firstborn characteristics in yourself, etc.?
4. How could parents help their children not fall into the stereotyped birth order roles?

Chapter 11

1. What are some common reasons siblings fight?
2. How could some of these fights be avoided?
3. When do problems between siblings become dangerous rather than just normal sibling quarrels?
4. If you had a friend who told you her brother was abusing her, what advice would you give her?

Chapter 12

1. Can you think of an example of a fight you had with a sibling this week and what caused it?
2. How could it have been avoided or what solutions would have worked?
3. What are some keys to getting along better with siblings?
4. How could families work together to improve sibling relationships? What role should the parents take?